The Anatomy of Knowledge

The Anatomy of Knowledge & the Ontological Necessity of First Principles

KARIM LAHHAM

TABAH RESEARCH

CLASSIFICATION OF THE SCIENCES PROJECT TABAH PAPERS SERIES | NUMBER 1 | 2021

The Anatomy of Knowledge and the Ontological Necessity of First Principles

ISBN: 978-9948-8607-0-9

All praise is to Allah alone, the Lord of the Worlds
And may He send His benedictions upon
our master Muḥammad, his Kin
and his Companions
and grant them
peace

Summary

This paper in the series explores one of the first principles of metaphysics, the principle of identity in its logical form, namely, the principle of non-contradiction, and the relationship between its metaphysical and logical dimensions. It is invariably the task of revelation to provide definable and recognizable references that can be brought into human understanding. Logic is given the role of providing in us an eternal order reflective of the order of creation, a role that bestows upon it, therefore, a certain sacrality. The Kantian conceptualist contention, now often encountered, establishes the basis for the contemporary de-ontologization of logic, since it creates a split between second intentions and first intentions, ensuring that reality has no input into the workings of the mind. Secondary intelligibles, however, are based on first intelligibles – things that exist – and thus they are ontologically dependent and reflective of that order. The logical thus can never contradict the metaphysical, and the metaphysical can never in turn be illogical. This seamlessness between the two orders is critical to the safeguarding of a sound intellectual discourse enabling the human soul to understand its existential condition, a condition that remains the same regardless of time and place.

About the Author

KARIM LAHHAM, MA (RCA), MA (OXON.), PHD (CANTAB.), Barrister-at-law of the Inner Temple. He is the author of, *inter alia*, *The Roman Catholic Church's Position on Islam After Vatican II* and *'Being Good': An Ontological View of Ethics*.

الْعِلْمُ النَّافِعُ هُوَ الَّذِي يَنْبَسِطُ فِي الصَّدْرِ شُعَاعُهُ،
وَيَنْكَشِفُ بِهِ عَنِ الْقَلْبِ قِنَاعُهُ

*Beneficial knowledge is that whose ray of light expands in
the breast and by which is uncovered the heart's veil.*
— Ibn ʿAṭāʾillāh, *Ḥikam*, no. 231.

Contents

Preface to the Series

THE PAPERS INAUGURATED in this new series are essentially an exercise in conceptual disambiguation relating to the central problem of what could be termed cognitive hierarchy, and the role and implication of principled thought to the *turāth*. The intent was not so much to present an academic exercise in erudite prose but rather to engage ideas around the consequences of presuming a classification of the sciences in order to catalyse a persuasive discourse on pedagogical protocols, on the framing of a modernist refurbishment of the religious sciences, and the centrality and need for the rooting of all intellectual adventures in first principles. There is nothing new essentially in these essays, in as far as one could say that the bricks and mortar of a building are nothing new, but what is presented represents perhaps a new architectural resolution as to how those same bricks and mortar may be utilized more effectively.

The Classification of the Sciences Project was initiated in late 2015 at Tabah Research, a division of Tabah Foundation. Having expended ten years since its inauguration in disseminating lectures and studies, researchers at the Foundation came to have a clearer idea of the state of contemporary intellectual discourse in the Islamic world, predominantly in relation to the religious sciences. What effectively came to notice was that much of the confusion surrounding adherence to traditional models of education revolved around a correct understanding of traditional hierarchies that necessitated certain pedagogical methodologies. The commissioning of this project arose due to several reasons. Foremost among those was the spread of modernist secularist viewpoints in relation to education and traditional knowledge. Despite the many advantages and benefits of the universal model of university education of the last century, one can scarcely avoid its connection with an increase in latitudinarian attitudes to knowledge, or, one can say, the democratization of knowledge. It is safe to say that access to university or school education is not the same as access to knowledge. Furthermore, the accumulation and learning of facts can never be synonymous with, nor amount to, scientific knowledge.[1] In contrast, knowledge in the traditional model is attained through principles that govern the relationship of things, the order of things. Moreover, the underlying structure of metaphysics that imbues all theoretical knowledge ensures that the fetidness of reason can never strangulate transcendent aspirations, as metaphysics ensures that the framework of knowledge belongs to *theoria*, ensuring the necessity of vision for the completion or perfection of the cognitive process.

On a more foundational note, the animating principles of the project stem unashamedly from the complete metaphysical acceptance of the Ash'ari creed, despite the unconventional manner in which it might be presented, and an unqualified adherence to the school of Imam Junayd in *iḥsān*. The contemporary waning of the Ash'ari creed in many intellectual circles due to the general and modernist recoil from such central and critical ideas has largely not been ameliorated. The recent attempt to stem such a credal desuetude by way of a reactionary and muscular neo-Ash'arism has led to a dangerous rationalization of *'aqīda* more befitting the ambience of a wrestling pit and its corresponding etiquette, rather than the sober scholarly forum demanded by the subject matter.

The authority of pedagogical methodologies in the transmission of the Islamic sciences is another point in question that has led to much pondering. Once again, much ink has been spilt on whether traditional methodologies should 'keep up with the times', or adhere to more critical and historicist positions, or even be abolished. The question that could be distilled from such abundant objections is the one that asks whether traditional methodologies of transmission were necessarily part and parcel of the discipline being inculcated, and thus sacrosanct at their core, or whether they were merely incidental and of practical significance alone. That is to say, whether one can separate transmission procedure from substantive knowledge. The answer to this question and the manner in which it is answered necessarily determines the future of the Islamic intellectual sciences.

We contend that any discourse on these aforesaid matters must be based on, understand, and commit to metaphysical coherence. By this we mean that sound discourse must be in line with metaphysical principles, being themselves reflections of the order of Reality. The first paper in the series explores one of those first principles of metaphysics, the principle of identity in its logical form, namely, the principle of non-contradiction, and the relationship between its metaphysical and logical dimensions.

The second paper explores the nature of definition and whether the latter is effective in advancing conceptual knowledge that may be deemed essential or objective. The third paper examines the notion of objectivity by setting out the various understandings of the theory of *nafs al-amr*, or things in themselves. If reason is relational, then how do we situate and come to know the object of our thought in itself shorn of that subjective relationality?

The truth and how we arrive at it in the Islamic intellectual tradition provide the main focus of the first three papers. The centrality of the role of the sciences in treating the various levels of reality is purported to be key to understanding the necessity for hierarchy, and if hierarchy, then order of knowledge. Every intellectual perception is subject to a science, that is to say, it pertains to a science in the order of knowledge. Just as reality is multilateral in its aspects, so is knowledge, in that one may speak of a direct correlation between levels of existence or reality and levels of knowledge. This is a cosmological truth as well as a metaphysical truth, as the world can never be known simply as one-dimensional in the traditional perspective. The symbolic frame of mind, necessary to any serious metaphysical work, arises from a vision of the universe as wheels within wheels, intertwined and interrelated dimensions revealing a synthetic unity that ensures continuity of theological meaning. It is to see things in reality in their unitive rather than in their separative aspects. This viewpoint sees the world as metaphysically transparent, a place that may be sifted for the understanding of the qualities and attributes of God, and thus allowing us to put everything in its place, and more importantly, to see everything in its rightful place.

The realm of reason is essential to understanding and situating the realm of the *'aqliyyāt*, wherein the three foundational papers in the series can be situated. Just as the truths of reason can never be incompatible with the Qur'ān and Sunna, we can safely say that the truths of the Qur'ān and Sunna can never be unreasonable. Having said that, reason naturally plays a mediating role for truths but up to a point, since it is the passivity of the intellect that ensures the higher echelons of cognitive capacity. The use of logic is determinant of sound discourse and essential for the determination of sound judgements. Logic, however, is largely a methodology, a tool, rather than knowledge per se, one that validates the process of thought but cannot create the content of thought. One must first therefore have something on which logic can work, a premise from which one might proceed. Its basis thus lies in metaphysics, and because there is no break in reality, the rational is premised on Reality, not only extramental reality as generally understood.

The logical thus can never contradict the metaphysical, and the metaphysical can never in turn be illogical. This seamlessness between the two orders is critical to the safeguarding of a sound intellectual discourse representing no less than a principial underpinning of logic by metaphysics. Although invariably the truths of metaphysics are imposed upon us, much as Reality is imposed upon us, the intellectual realm is there to allow us to expose those truths, uncovering and discovering them by principial deliberation or insight. It is in this way that every age must call for a return to principle, if it is to safeguard the ability for the human soul to understand its existential condition, a condition that remains the same regardless of time and place.

Karim Lahham (Series Editor)
Oxford
19 January 2021

IN THE NAME OF GOD, THE MERCIFUL, THE BENEFICENT

The Anatomy of Knowledge & the Ontological Necessity of First Principles

THIS PAPER intends to examine the relationship between the order of knowledge and its principles, and the justification for such an order. The intention is to take one aspect of this epistemic structure, as expressed in Avicennian and post-Avicennian thought, namely, the first principle of non-contradiction, in order to examine its priority and primacy. The context of the paper is to rebut the contemporary dissipation of the notion of the hierarchy of the sciences, leading some to think that traditional methodologies of transmission are outdated and based on customary practices alone that enshrine social and thought control on behalf of a particular caste. Contrary to this we contend that the order of knowledge is reflective of the order of being, by way of intellectual and ontological necessity and not due to any imposed system from without. This imposes, though, from within, a transmission process that determines the prerequisites for the study of the sciences.

It has been a literary custom of the last hundred years or so for traditionalist writers to preface their purported corrective treatises or essays with the declaration that such work is disseminated in the hope of rectifying the cognitive errors of an age mired in intellectual and moral confusion.[2] The implication being that once the errors were understood or highlighted, it was optimistically held that an intellectual reassessment might then be undertaken by a bona fide reader, or that at the very least former positions might be interrogated. The problem, however, may not lie simply in the supine demeanour of the reader or in their sultry passivity. There has also, and very often, been a recognizable deficit in historical orientation in such studies in relation to contemporary approaches to modern ideas assailing the Muslim world. Without an element of historical sophistication, there is an undeniable tendency to distort intellectual perspectives on the present, a mistaking of old facts and old theories for new, leading ultimately, and perhaps inevitably, to an inability to evaluate the significance of new movements and methodologies. We aver that the history of an idea and its philosophical foundation and antecedent forms is a significant part of the cognitive structure that permits us to understand the questions or *masā'il* of a science, an understanding that remains incomplete if it relies merely on an existential study of those questions.

It is noticeable that the Islamic world's traditional cognitive systems have further deteriorated to a very great extent in the last two decades, so that it may be said that the nefarious force arraigned before traditional thought amounts to intellectual sedition, rather than mere intellectual error. By sedition is meant an active incitement on the part of a not insignificant minority to foment intellectual rebellion and disorder against and within the guardians and defenders of traditional religious authority and knowledge. The distinction between error and sedition is important because it implies that the rejection of traditional thought, or traditional foundationalism, by contemporary antagonists primarily is a psychological imposture rather than an intellectual deviation. Such a rejection is largely made not because such respective thought is false, but rather because it is falsely known. Epistemologically speaking, the accession to human knowledge is also a psychological operation, and therefore studied under epistemology, that is to say, incorporating the study of the vegetative, sensitive, and intellectual operations and faculties.

Rejecting metaphysics or the science of first principles, as contemporary modern thought tends to do, in the name of a suspect scepticism has long been the result of a psychological inclination rather than any misspent search for demonstrative and objective truth. It is itself incidentally a metaphysical act and can never be considered metaphysically neutral. Good faith can go a long way in the preparation of minds, so that one could even say that it is possible for an ignorant man to be a virtuous man, but it does not then follow that ignorance can ever amount to a virtue. The uncritical adoption of neo-positivist natural sciences and their attendant philosophical outlooks in the present context of the Islamic world is symptomatic of a universal tendency that has spread irrespective of creed, belief, or theological affiliation.

By reiterating the importance of psychological disposition there is no intention to give further credibility to the intellectually unsound tenets of modern psychology. We are not suggesting that the laws of logic are furnished by psychology, rather that they are objective laws that impose themselves on us, and therefore also on our psychology.[3] Their acceptance thus, subjectively speaking, is dependent to a certain significant extent on personal disposition, but their validity, objectively speaking, can never be.

It is this that separates our perspective from that of modern proponents of psychologism in logic. In terms of analysing a proposition, to take a more concrete example, its psychological treatment is distinguished from the logical as the latter can only subject it to an analysis if it possesses the traits of necessity and universal validity.

Acts and beliefs in the traditional order are always posited on an intelligible and logical order that underpins them and are capable of being understood and analysed even if the act in question may prima facie appear illogical and unconscious. By psychological disposition, rather, we necessarily also infer a moral valuation, as there is an essential relation between thought and action, and consequently between intellection and morality. The moral or immoral act has a direct effect on the human powers of intellection, and vice versa. To think as one pleases, rather than to think correctly, may be an intellectual error, but we further contend must also be necessarily a moral imposture as it prioritises caprice before intellect. In this context, one could be excused for thinking the signature of the modern age to be characterized as a noisy clamour for liberty for the many, merely in order to secure licence for the few.

One of the many significant and malefic acts of early modern philosophy, one that can be said to animate and inform contemporary thought as a whole, was the denial of the passivity of the human intellect. Immanuel Kant, especially although not exclusively, advanced this in pursuit of the ideology of the freedom of thought, an ideology that believed that the mind must think itself as independent and self-sufficient in its creative powers.[4] Kant essentially operated a 'secret axiom', namely, that we only know what we ourselves construct.[5] Subjection to truth, however, according to traditional metaphysics demands a passivity of mind, illustrating that the intellect is not then free to think what it pleases, but only free to think the truth. This is not to deny that the intellect acts, as it clearly does, but it cannot act unless it has itself been acted upon. This is important because it touches upon the most basic epistemological question, namely, whether the mind is able to think before it has been given something to think about. Can the intellect in those circumstances think at all? The answer should be determinedly clear, as only the Divine Intellect can be independently creative and active. The human intellect consequently is not free to think what it pleases.

By moral we also mean a spiritual concomitant rather than merely an ethical standard, for in the traditional order, the ethical is never detached from spiritual composure. *Adab*, unlike superficial piety, is at the core of the learning process as attested by numerous treatises and the continuity of the traditional culture of learning in the madrasa system. What al-Ghazālī and others referred to as *tahdhīb al-akhlāq*, the refinement of character, is deemed by someone like Quṭb al-Dīn al-Shīrāzī to be a necessary prerequisite for the study of logic. He states, for example, in the opening remarks of his *Commentary* on *Ḥikmat al-Ishrāq* that: 'those who do not refine their character and purify their dispositions (*aʿrāq*) before undertaking the study of logic have launched themselves on the course of miscreance (*manhaj al-ḍalāl*) and are engaged on the path of the ignorant (*silk al-juhhāl*).'[6] These sentiments are by no means an anomaly, but rather are repeated throughout *ishrāqī* texts as well as those texts following the Akbarian School, namely, that the epistemic act demands a spiritual prerequisite.

One can say that there are ultimately two systems of thought or philosophy, those that find reality ultimately meaningful and intelligible, and those that do not. Traditional Islamic thought belongs to the former, as it adheres in its creed to the intelligibility of reality, and if intelligible, then capable of being known. This acceptance of intelligibility presumes common presuppositions in the order of knowledge, as the common form of metaphysics in the Islamic intellectual tradition underpins such an order. The division of the sciences and the necessary consequence of a hierarchical interconnectedness between them necessarily underwrite this. This matter will therefore be examined first.

The intention here, then, is not to furnish a mere historical catalogue of the varying taxonomies found in Islamic intellectual history. Rather, the primary purpose is to set out the principles by which the parameters of each science and their requisite boundaries and competences are established as a window onto the structure of knowledge and objective reality. The basic reasoning behind this is twofold. The modern West has since the time of the Renaissance sacrificed its understanding of the unity of science for the universality of science. The price of universality, however, led to the dilution of the boundaries between the sciences on the basis that such boundaries were nominal rather than real distinctions, accidental rather than *de re*. The intellectual link between the nominalism of figures such as Nicolas d'Autrécourt in the fourteenth century and the later naturalist impasse in Western philosophical history is now unquestionable.[7] Secondly, the uncritical adoption of positivist natural sciences has now become a universal phenomenon irrespective of creed or theological school. This questionable but unquestioned practice must either be due to the lack of a corresponding natural philosophy to counter its claims, or due to the inability to see its positioning as incompatible with traditional metaphysics.

The focus thus is precisely on the inter-relationality and individual competence of the speculative sciences due to the incumbent crisis of the built environment and ecological disfunctionality of much of the modern world. The pursuit of solutions to these problems in the tortuous valleys of politics and instrumental problem-solving methodologies has proved futile. The seemingly intact nature of the authority of the religious sciences has not altered the picture either, implying that the problem does not arise simply in the authoritative structure of the religious sciences, but rather in the domain of the science of natural philosophy and its attendant subalternated sciences. The correct understanding of the hierarchy of the speculative sciences is also determinant of the role and supremacy of metaphysics and its handmaiden logic in situating the rest of the classificatory order. These subtle orders remain little taught or expounded, if at all, and are decontextualized from the necessary impact that they entail in the realm of the practical sciences. The unquestionable and unquestioned application of technology, itself a process rather than a science, reverts back to not merely a pronouncement of the science of ethics, but more importantly to a misunderstanding of the delimitation of natural philosophy.

The doctrinal presuppositions adhered to by us and in our approach are those of epistemological realism, but also cosmological realism. By the latter I mean that the created world is imbued with reality, and thus with meaning, and that this meaning has correspondences in other realms of reality. This correspondence means that nothing can be isolated from everything else. The created world is not one-dimensional, a static entity that is passively present for one to assert or foist upon it one's own thoughts, prejudices, and desires. Rather, and from our perspective, it is a reality that is ordered and suffused with effective and active meaningful symbolic activity. In general philosophical terms, however, realism is essentially the acceptance of the primacy of being over thought. The second presupposition of epistemological realism we hold maintains that the content of thought is obtained from extramental reality through the primary perception of the senses. The mode in which this content is known is the mode of universality due to the activity of the intellect, which in turn provides the objects of thought with a mode of existence referred to as intentional existence. The third presupposition is that being is intelligible, and thus all that is in existence is intelligible, and the perfection of intelligibility is truth. In this way we can therefore assert that being and truth are convertible.

We also propose to set out the principal assertion that logical truth is distinguished from ontological truth but cannot be separated from it. When we say ontological, we intend the truth in things, and when we say logical, we intend the truth of things. The two orders, in other words, are interconnected. Given that Reality is one, the order of being, we say, imposes itself on the order of thought and intellect, giving the order of being a primacy that cannot be usurped. Furthermore, we intend to show, however concisely, that the necessity of the order of being in turn brings forth the reality of logical necessities. In this vein, the principle of non-contradiction and other such axioms cannot be considered laws of propositions *simpliciter.*

The paper will, following the above, be composed of three main sections. The first represents an answer to the ontological question, what are first principles and what is the context in which they are situated, namely, within the anatomy of the classificatory structure of the sciences? The second is an attempt to answer the epistemological question of how we come to know a first principle and its constituent parts and formulation. The third will examine the answer to the teleological question of the purpose of the first principle and its implication, philosophically and cosmologically, specifically in the context of the principle of non-contradiction. The three answers are merely concise attempts to frame the wider issue of the hierarchy of traditional knowledge systems and its necessary relationship to the order of nature in the face of a latitudinarian modernist assault.

The Ontological Dimension

The Division of the Sciences and Its Principles

The metaphysical approach takes its starting point in the Absolutely Real and not in created things. The starting point is, in other words, the

Absolute, working down towards the contingent, and not working up from contingency to the Real. This is the modus operandi of metaphysical thinking, hence the ontological priority in this paper's methodology. This is mirrored by Ibn 'Aṭā'illāh when he states:[8]

> What a difference between one who proceeds from God in his argumentation and one who proceeds inferentially to Him! He who has Him as his starting point knows the Real (*al-Ḥaqq*) as It is, and proves any matter by reference to the being of its Origin. But inferential argumentation comes from the absence of union with Him. Otherwise, when was it that He was absent that one has to proceed inferentially to Him? Or when was it that He was distant that created things (*al-āthār*) themselves will unite us to Him?

Having said that, arguments or statements of theory in any field presuppose the principles of logic. All arguments, therefore, are logical in the sense that they must pertain to logical rules, but not necessarily in the sense that they are fabricated out of logical principles and terms. Logic is a tool that furnishes the method for all science and hence is traditionally studied prior to any other science, because it verifies and examines the instruments used by all other sciences. The intellectual sciences, however, require a contextualization and delimitation that can only be fully realized through the process of a hierarchical ordering.

A word should be said about choosing to focus on a classificatory system that is essentially Avicennian in structure, and one that figures largely, albeit implicitly but skeletally, in the post-Avicennian logical tradition. What is meant here is that the tripartite division of the speculative sciences, dependent on the order of being, cannot change in its core from one classificatory system to another except by way of expression. It is superfluous to mention (except for the sake of clarification) that Ibn Sīnā's classification allows a wider picture of integration of all the sciences than, say, the *kalām* expositions of classification by Fakhr al-Dīn al-Rāzī. The reorganization of the classification of the sciences by Rāzī might be interpreted as an attempt to dismantle the epistemic interconnectedness of the structure of the sciences that Ibn Sīnā's classification had revealed. One could rather say that it was more an attempt to reorder the sciences by reducing the study of physics and metaphysics largely to principles, amounting simply to an integration of those sciences into *kalām*, albeit the main focus being at times more on the classification of existents, substances, and accidents.[9] This does not, however, pose a significant problem in trying to rebut the incoherence of positivist science and its reduction of all science to its model and discourse, nor does it amount to the denial of the interconnectedness of all knowledge. Further difficulties may be in store if Rāzī's *via moderna* is to be interpreted as a model by scholars such as Eichner, who frames Rāzī's approach in the following way.

> This classification, however, leaves no space to integrate more specialized scientific disciplines of the Greek canon. Paradoxically, we may identify the comprehensive and systematic character of these encyclopaedic expositions as a considerable obstacle for developing an epistemological theory that can integrate specialized scientific disciplines into a coherent framework. Disciplines like ethics, political science, or mathematics and astronomy, or medicine are not integrated in the framework of the program of Post-Avicennian philosophical disciplines.
>
> In the case of some disciplines, rudimentary basics are dealt with in this encyclopaedic context. However, the encyclopaedic character prevents a more detailed investigation of these topics. Thus, rudimentary cosmological sketches form part of most expositions, likewise the theory of the elements and the basics of humoral pathology. The presence of these topics in philosophical works and, from the 13th century onwards, in *kalām* works is typically interpreted as pointing to a close relation between rationalist traditions among Islamic theologians and science. The relation, however, is to be evaluated in a more nuanced way: When theological expositions mention some basic information on scientific theories this certainly may show that theologians were not hostile towards discussing these theories, but this did not necessarily imply that they possessed a serious scientific command of the relevant disciplines.[10]

The 'encyclopaedic' works she is referring to are those such as Abharī's *Hidāya* and Kātibī's *Ḥikmat al-ʿAyn*,[11] which one can say are far from being encyclopaedic. Furthermore, a cursory glance at Ījī's *Risālat al-Akhlāq,* Abharī's *Hidāya,* or Ṭūsī's *Akhlāq-i Naṣīrī* may be sufficient to dispel this contention regarding the post-Avicennian intellectual landscape by their evident portrayal of an implicit integrative model that is precisely underpinned by a strict ontological observance of the interconnectedness of the sciences.

Gutas interprets this purported shift as an attempt to harness the non-theological sciences to a disingenuous apologetical agenda to further theological dogma. There is an alternative, and perhaps more charitable, view, in that the shift was an attempt to concentrate on the essential elements that serve soteriological values. This may refer to the *kalām* treatises *per se* but does not mean more scientific treatises ceased to be penned or deemed unimportant by those same authors. One worrisome development, though, that Gutas highlights is a creeping atomization of the science of logic, formerly closely treated with metaphysics.[12] However, if the subject matter is accepted to be secondary intelligibles, which in the said period of atomization remains the case, then this can only be so because there is a rootedness of logic in metaphysics. It is sufficiently difficult therefore to understand Gutas's and Eichner's contentions as representative of a widespread disassociation of metaphysics from other sciences, a disassociation that brought about untold misery and horror to the Western world, as well as heralding the modernist viewpoint.

The traditional viewpoint, which we espouse in contrast to the modernist, views every science as a system of knowledge having for its object an aspect of reality, essentially 'divisions' and 'species' of *wujūd.* This is due to each of the speculative sciences having as its subject the study of the existent from a particular vantage point, that is to say, a differing formal object. Only metaphysics, given its subject matter, can lay claim that its material object is the same as its formal object. If every science views reality from a particular vantage point, they are also each a whole and pertain to a unity, a unity that is neither numerical nor logical, but metaphysical. The difference here is that a unity based on a mathematical term 'one' belongs to the genus of quantity, a genus that is limited to material things alone. The term 'one' in metaphysics, however, is not restricted to a genus, but applies to all things that exist. In logic, a genus is that which is arrived at by the abstraction of the differences that exist between two or more species of being, that is to say, it leaves out the differences. Logical unity thus refers to the order of essence, the unity of the essence in the mind shorn of the differences. Metaphysical unity can be distinguished from logical unity, in that the latter demands an exclusion of differences, whereas the former is a unity that is inclusive of the differences that we find in the *a'yān fī al-khārij* (things in external manifestation). The foundation for this unity and the interrelationship of one science with another is therefore necessarily dependent on the understanding of the ontological ground for the three speculative sciences.[13]

As was intimated above, metaphysics is the universal science that investigates the ground and basis of all reality, precisely universal because it investigates that which is common to all reality, seeking the ultimate unity and ground of all reality, the Absolute. It is essential therefore to draw out some inferences[14] at this stage if we are to take metaphysics seriously. As we shall see further below, the subject of metaphysics is being qua being, and as such is the supreme science that does not rely upon, nor subordinate itself to, any other science. As Aristotle pointed out, being is predicated of everything and cannot serve to distinguish between one kind of thing from another. He also states that every science concerns a single genus unified by a common property, but metaphysics is the exception, as being is not a genus (*jins*) and cannot have differentia (*faṣl*). The reason for this is that a genus or differentia implies a logical operation of exclusion and inclusion, which in the case of existence is absurd as existence is all-inclusive. Consequent to this, existence cannot be defined, nor even described, as there is nothing clearer or more evident than it.

What can be considered the method of metaphysics following upon this and how does it arrive at its starting point? Is it the use of reasoning? Reasoning is mediated knowledge that naturally depends on pre-existing knowledge. Reasoning utilizes syllogisms, and syllogisms proceed from and presuppose premises that are certain. Reasoning may be said to be the attempt to reach a judgement through certain means when the judgement cannot be arrived at directly. When the intellect is unable to elicit the agreement or disagreement between two ideas, it brings in a third idea which has a relation to the two ideas in order to be able to make a judgement. The syllogism is the instrument of this form of deductive reasoning, which is composed of three propositions. Its method of operation is that when the first two are given, the premises (*al-muqaddimāt*), the third follows as a matter of necessity, as the conclusion (*al-maṭlūb*) exists in the premises. When John Stuart Mill stated that the syllogism was useless on the basis that the conclusion must be known prior to articulating the premises (a *petitio principii*) and that it provides no new knowledge, he was mistaken on both counts.[15] In the first place, the conclusion cannot be explicitly known prior to the premises, but is implicitly present as stated earlier, and may be explicitly deduced from the premises. Secondly, although new knowledge may not necessarily be arrived at by way of the syllogism, the latter does furnish a clearer and more explicit knowledge.

Returning to metaphysics as the supreme science, this primacy entails that it refer back to an immediate self-evident truth, as it cannot take any postulates or principles from any other science. It cannot, however, also take its starting point from a principle, such as the principle of identity: A is A; whatever is, is. Although this is a fundamental first principle, it nevertheless cannot be the starting point of metaphysics. It is true that whatever is, certainly is, but it cannot answer the question of whether something is or not, nor can it tell us anything about reality. Even if the principle were to contain all that metaphysics needs as a starting point, the devolvement of the principle would require the use of logic to unfurl its content. This would also presuppose the laws of logic by metaphysics, which represents an impasse. If the starting point of metaphysics were to be from principle, then it would be difficult to avoid an inevitable essentialism, confining metaphysics to the realm of essences, even ideas, rather than real being.

An analytic methodology that is deductive, as shown above, cannot provide us with the starting point of metaphysics. This is the taking of a self-evident principle as the starting point of metaphysics. Aristotle in his *Posterior Analytics* says as much when he states that if one is appealing to principles in order to explain first principles then one is inviting circularity.[16] It is on this basis that he denies that metaphysics can be thought of as a demonstrative science. This really goes to the reason why the method of metaphysics is an important question to resolve, given that demonstration cannot be considered a valid method here.[17]

It can also be safely ascertained that an inductive methodology would scarcely satisfy as a solution. This is apart from the fact that mere observation or sense experience of something would inductively only produce probable knowledge, not certain knowledge, and would thus fall short of the certainty that metaphysics demands. The process of induction, however, cannot be presupposed by metaphysics as the first science; therefore, induction must be vindicated through induction in order to qualify. This leads effectively to circularity.

If reasoning or observation cannot produce the starting point of metaphysics, does this inevitably lead to a denial of metaphysics? If the starting point cannot be demonstrated, does that mean there can be no reliance on it? What is certain is that a rejection of metaphysics would imply indubitably a contradiction between the denial and the means of the denial, namely, the act of rejection itself.[18] One cannot therefore deny metaphysics, nor seemingly, and paradoxically, affirm it demonstratively. Principally, and in resolution of the conundrum, we contend that metaphysics is necessarily 'experiential' at the outset rather than deductive or inductive, and that this experience above all concerns a relation with Being, a consciousness, which is indubitably certain. This is again the major difference between what may be termed philosophy and metaphysics. Philosophy begins with doubt and follows an intellectual process to arrive at certainty. Metaphysics begins with certainty and proceeds to certainty. Following upon this, one can extrapolate that since knowing must necessarily be conditioned by being, metaphysics is foremost a lived experience, then subsequently expressed in an intellectual form. It is this experience, in the sense of consciousness not sense experience, which gives rise to the first principle of identity and its negative correlative, the principle of non-contradiction, which will be examined below.

The classification of the sciences arises from the knowledge structure that Ibn Sīnā establishes, namely, that knowledge concerns two domains, *taṣawwur* (primary apprehension, concept) and *taṣdīq* (judgement). These also represent two orders of knowledge, each reducing themselves to primary notions or concepts in the order of *taṣawwur*, and first principles in propositional form in the order of *taṣdīq*. This understanding is the basis of the hierarchy of the sciences, in that, as per Aristotle, each science concerns an organized body of knowledge that is properly known through demonstration (*burhān*). The sciences treat of changing phenomena, but must state a truth that is changeless.[19] The foundations for this demonstrative process are the primary propositions, in turn built on primary notions. Each science relies on postulates or principles that are prior to the science itself in an ascending order of hierarchy, much as propositions and concepts reduce respectively to first principles and primary notions, reaching an apex representing metaphysics. Science therefore cannot be restricted to one genus, and correspondingly there must then be a set of principles relating to each genus of things. It is on these principles that method depends.

One may of course question the primacy of metaphysics, since the use of logical operations such as reduction and deduction in metaphysical discourse seems to suggest that their validity is taken for granted by metaphysics. This is evidently incongruous, or even incompatible, with the position of metaphysics as a supreme science. One could also say that both logic and metaphysics share in a general sense the same subject matter. This view, once again, would be broadly true, except for the important distinction that the subject of metaphysics is more precisely being qua being, whereas that of logic is being qua knowledge of being. As was stated earlier, metaphysics cannot take the validity of any operation as said or for granted. Primarily, one can say that metaphysics is prior to logic, as shown above. This priority is logically and ontologically necessarily so. However, the starting point of metaphysics, the experience of *wujūd*, gives rise to questions, such as whether a thing is existent or non-existent. This question, and even the rational structure of the question, sets the conditions of the possibility of thinking of, and about, the question itself, through the application of the method of reduction. Moreover, deduction would necessitate the conformation of our thinking to the laws of logic, the latter simultaneously appearing with metaphysics, or as soon as metaphysics becomes intellectually operative. This does not, however, readily permit the idea that logic would ever enter constitutively into the proof of a metaphysical proposition, since, strictly speaking, logic cannot be prior to metaphysics. If thus understood, logic enters, then, only as a necessary tool for the organization of the evidence bearing upon the said metaphysical proof.

After this framing, which will be subsequently enlarged upon, we propose in the following section to explore a particular structural aspect of classification, albeit one that originates in Aristotle's *Posterior Analytics,* but which has been incorporated into the Islamic logical tradition largely through Ibn Sīnā's *Kitāb al-burhān* in his *Shifā'.* This aspect relates to the two central ideas discussed in the sphere of logic, namely, the rule of the prohibition of *metábasis* (*man' naql al-burhān*), and its partial exception, the theory of the subalternation of the sciences (*tadākhul al-'ulūm al-mutabāyina*).[20] These two ideas are to be explored through their averred implicit continuity in the *umūr 'āmma* and in the traditional unfolding of the apodictic sciences. It is in effect to explore the understanding of the relations between second intentions (*al-ma'qūlāt al-thāniya*) and first intentions (*al-ma'qūlāt al-ūlā*).

When we speak of the division of the sciences, we invoke a logical operation that serves a similar function to that of definition. Division (*taqsīm*) is not enumeration, but a marking of the boundaries of the denotation of the sciences. It is sometimes described as denotative definition, putting forward the extension of a term in order to denote the particulars that may be subsumed within a class. This is in contrast to definition which is concerned with comprehending the term or analysing the concept it refers to. In division, one begins with a genus and then divides it into the particular classes of which it is composed arriving at species. Classification (*tartīb*) operates in reverse and begins with particulars and ascends from there to the genus, where certain classes are grouped together and are brought within a larger class. So 'sheep', 'horse', 'donkey', and 'cow' are particulars that can be classified under the genus 'animal'. The higher class in terms of classificatory ascendance can only be identified through division, so in effect the two logical operations of division and definition are essentially complementary.

A. ARISTOTELIAN ORIGINS

The treatment of the two ideas of metabasis and subalternation referred to earlier originate in the first book of the *Posterior Analytics*. Aristotle discusses there the nature of a demonstrative science, scientific knowledge (*epistasthai*) being known through demonstration (*apodeixis*). What he means to say by this is that it consists of a deduction that entails the necessary truth of its conclusion and makes known the grounds (*aitia*) for such a conclusion.[21] Whether a valid deduction is a demonstration will naturally depend on the premises. A demonstrative scientific knowledge depends on things that are (1) true, (2) primary (i.e. indemonstrable), (3) immediate (*amesos*),[22] (4) more intelligible than, (5) prior to, and (6) explanatory of the conclusion.[23] All propositions of science must satisfy the first requirement, but only principles are also primary and immediate.[24] Any propositions used as premises in a demonstration must satisfy requirements 1, as stated above, but in addition 4–6. Only a premise that can satisfy all six requirements is considered a principle (*archē*). But a premise need not satisfy all the requirements, as that would not allow a conclusion to serve as a premise.[25] A principle of a demonstration is what is primary, and an immediate proposition, one to which no other proposition is prior.[26] Thus we arrive at the cardinal rule that since all scientific knowledge depends on primary and immediate propositions, it depends on principles. These principles although knowable are indemonstrable (*anapodeikton*), but nevertheless are still subject to a negative demonstration by a *reductio ad absurdum* consisting in showing that there is a dependence without exception on their assumption.[27]

There are three categories of principles according to Aristotle, namely, (1) axioms that are common (*koina*) principles occurring in more than one science, (2) definitions (*horismos*, pl. *horoi*) of the subject and attributes of the science in question, which are considered as proper (*idia*) to each respective science, and (3) assertions that the subject of the science in question exists, which are also considered as proper principles.[28]

The subject genus of a science, what it is about, is the basis for the proper principles of a science. Each science treats of one genus; for example, metaphysics treats the genus of being, as it were, and thus all the causes related to being. This singularity serves as a principle of identity for each respective science.[29] Following on this, since different sciences have different genera, a demonstration whose terms all belong to the same genus of that particular science cannot have a conclusion whose terms are from another genus. Such a conclusion would necessarily be irrelevant to the science in question. A conclusion would have to contain two of the terms found in the premises. The terms of a demonstration according to Aristotle, to claim to *be* a demonstration, must be related *per se* rather than *per accidens* to the genus of the science it belongs to. This means that all the terms that appear in its premises and conclusions belong to the same genus. A demonstration whose terms belong to a genus of a particular science cannot have a conclusion whose terms are from the genus of another science.[30] If a term is *per accidens*, then there is no demonstration, because unless all the terms of a demonstration are from the same genus, the demonstration would contain terms that are accidentally rather than essentially related. The rule of the prohibition of *metabasis* can therefore be enunciated as the prohibition of allowing scientific demonstrations to cross from one genus to another, the raison d'être being that such an act would be a category mistake, allowing terms to be applied *per accidens* rather than essentially and particularly.[31]

Each science in the Aristotelian classification can be said to correspond to a natural division of reality, but nevertheless all sciences come into being through definition.[32] Since the subject of a science is an aspect of reality with which the science is directly concerned, science cannot therefore be restricted to one genus, as no science can treat all problems. Each science is therefore a partial system, with a subject matter, a set of principles, and a method of its own.[33] The subalternate sciences are the only exception to the prohibition of genus crossing in demonstrations. For Aristotle, non-accidental knowledge, scientific knowledge, takes place when the middle terms belong to the same genus as the premises and the conclusion.[34] For a demonstration to be capable of being transferred from one science to another, the genera of the two sciences must be identical either unqualifiedly so or qualifiedly.[35] The examples he gives as an exception are that geometrical demonstrations apply to mechanical or optical demonstrations, and arithmetical demonstrations to harmonic demonstrations.[36]

A subalternate science is that which is primarily dependent on, or subordinate to, a superior science for its proofs and principles.[37] In the first example given by Aristotle, the subject genera of the sciences of geometry and optics are the same. Euclidean optics considered, the two sciences have common geometrical (spatial) properties so that their subject genera may be said to be the same. What Aristotle in effect was saying was that the two sciences had in common the same *modus considerandi*,[38] which is that which determines the structure, organization, and approach used in the proofs of the science.[39]

Aristotle further distinguishes between knowledge of a fact (*hoti*),[40] the domain of the subalternated science, and the knowledge of a reasoned fact (*dioti*),[41] that of the superior science.[42] A reasoned fact is knowledge of the fact together with an explanation, sometimes referred to as knowledge of the explanation rather than fact. In the relation of mathematics as superior science and harmonics as subalternate, the scientist working in harmonics knows the fact (the medieval *quia*), and the mathematician the demonstration of the explanation (*propter quid*). It may very well be that the mathematician may not know the particular fact, but only its explanation.[43]

In the science of harmonics, the scientist obtains facts empirically which he will then seek to find proofs for. These proofs will be found in the science of mathematics because of the manner in which he studies his science. If he does not do this, his knowledge would remain merely factual and would never be conclusively probative, since conclusions are to be found only in mathematics. He discovers the facts therefore as a scientist of harmonics but proves what he finds as a mathematician. The subalternate sciences for Aristotle are perceptual, whilst the superior sciences are mathematical, abstracted from the sensible world.[44] Their subject matter is different, and at one instance Aristotle avers that the subject genera of the two sciences may be different in contradiction to his own stated rule.[45] However, the dependence of the subordinated science on the superior rests in its reliance on the principles and proofs of the superior science. So once again, one studies sound qua numbers in the science of harmonics, and thus harmonics is subordinated to mathematics.

B. IBN SĪNĀ'S LEGACY

As a prefatory remark, it should be pointed out that we do not intend to recite the manner or history of the reception of the *Posterior Analytics* in the Avicennan tradition, nor to justify the legitimacy of demonstrative science within the wider theological tradition.[46] The role of metaphysics, together with its scope and function, remains the critical factor in situating the entire discourse of this paper. In this vein, the understanding of the hierarchy of values implicit in the order of the sciences is calibrated necessarily by the clarity with which the function of metaphysics is posited. The degree to which one may de-ontologize logic will also need to be explored below precisely to examine how this inevitably affects the legitimacy of the boundaries of the theoretical *ʿaqlī* sciences, and their relationship to metaphysics.[47] The differences between the theoretical sciences are peculiarities that are brought out in answer to the question of whether or not the subject matter can exist and be known independently of matter. The possibility of each science is dependent on the determination first of the subject matter (*mawḍūʿ*) and on its respective development of a method by which to reach the principles proper to it.

Ibn Sīnā does invariably incorporate the Aristotelian division of the sciences into his corpus, the difference, however, remaining in the manner in which he conceives the role of metaphysics. The discussion of classification takes place in five main places, *al-Madkhal*[48] being the first book of logic in the *Shifāʾ*, *al-Burhān*[49] the fifth book of logic in the *Shifāʾ*, *Kitāb al-najāt*,[50] *Kitāb al-ishārāt*,[51] and his *Risāla fī aqsām al-ʿulūm al-ʿaqliyya*.[52] This division of the sciences into theoretical and practical is a mainstay of every *kalām* textbook well into the later tradition most often as a *proemium*. The theoretical or speculative sciences for Ibn Sīnā unsurprisingly comprise three sciences, rather than the Aristotelian four:

natural philosophy (*al-ṭabī'ī*), which deals with mobile being; mathematics (*al-riyāḍī*), which relates to things that are dependent on sensible matter for their existence but not definition; and metaphysics (*al-ilāhī*), which studies being as being. It is well to note that the distinctions are conspicuously hierarchical and ontologically posited. All three theoretical sciences have derivative sciences under them or contained within each of them, respectively, for whom they furnish first principles. Once again, the distinction or separation of the sciences is premised on difference of genus.

If we look at mathematics, we find that the subject matter consists of numbers, points, lines, surfaces, and volumes. We find these matters also studied by the physicist, but as properties of physical bodies since they are contained in them as limits. Numbers, points, and so on cannot naturally exist extramentally apart from matter where they are subject to change. All things that are subject to change do so because they have matter, and it is the latter that undergoes change. The physicist studies this change as a fact, as physical forms always involve matter for their embodiment. This is bearing in mind that the subject matter as stated earlier in physics comprises bodies[53] that undergo change in size, quality, place, or substance, or move or stay fixed according to principle. Definition in this realm depends thus on matter. When we say physics, we include its possible subdivisions of biology and psychology. In mathematics, in contrast, definitions have no reference to matter capable of movement, so there can never be a proper definition of man in the science of mathematics. Numbers, points, and lines can be abstracted in thought and treated separately. The mathematician in effect investigates being qua quantitative and continuous.

Ibn Sīnā's *al-Burhān*, one of the nine books of logic in the *Shifā'*, has long been dismissed by scholars as a mere paraphrase of the *Posterior Analytics*, including much of what was set out above under Aristotle.[54] There are differences, however, and not just in the introduction of new subject chapters. At II.7, Ibn Sīnā, for example, introduces a discussion that deals with the relationship of the sciences and their subject matter, specifically discussing the distinction between metaphysics, dialectic (*jadal*), and sophistic (*sūfusṭā'iyya*).[55]

> First philosophy distinguishes itself from [dialectic and sophistic] in the starting point. For first philosophy takes its starting points from premises that are apodictic and certain

(*al-muqaddimāt al-burhāniyya al-yaqīniyya*). As to dialectic, its starting point is from premises that are truly generally known (*al-dhā'i'a*) and commonly accepted (*al-mashhūra*). As to sophistic, its starting point is from premises that seem to be generally known (*al-dhā'i'a*) or certain (*al-yaqīniyya*), but are not truly so.[56]

Every demonstrative science is deemed to have a subject matter (*mawḍū'*), principles (*mabādi'*), and questions (*masā'il*). As in Aristotle, the principles of a science are indemonstrable in the science within which they inhere,[57] but provable in a superior science. In the first *faṣl* of the opening chapter, Ibn Sīnā introduces the two apprehensions, namely, *taṣawwur* (known to the medieval West as *imaginatio*) and *taṣdīq* (*credulitas*), so that the first principle of a subject matter is to be arrived at through either *taṣawwurāt* (conceptualisations) – by way of real definitions (*ḥadd ḥaqīqī*) concerning the subject matter's essential attributes (*a'rāḍ dhātiyya*) – or *taṣdīqāt* (assents) arrived at by the syllogism (*qiyās*). Ibn Sīnā then proceeds to set out the notions of certainty and quasi-certainty in matters of belief. Certainty is the knowledge of something in a manner that does not admit of the possibility of contradiction. Uncertainty consequently is where the possibility of contradiction can be envisaged and must be considered.

The notion of certainty here does not admit of degrees as such, the gradation rather being the degree of conviction with which a person holds the truth. This is in line with his claim that *taṣdīq* comes in degrees, the highest being certainty (*yaqīn*), but this is considered a second order belief. Certainty comes with an accompanying second order belief (*yu'taqadu ma'ahu i'tiqādun thānin*), and it is this belief and its degree that determines the type of *taṣdīq*. The strength of this secondary belief is dependent on the awareness one may have of the strength of the first order belief, including the possibility of its contradictory being true.[58] Ibn Sīnā explains that a *taṣdīq* may be similar to certainty (*shabīh al-yaqīn*), but does not attain certainty precisely because of the strength of the secondary belief. This may be the case despite the fact that the near certain and the certain may be identical in terms of first order beliefs. Similarly, certainty can be diminished by the deterioration of a formerly held strong second order belief.[59] The *taṣdīq yaqīnī*, that which can be held with total certainty, is the first principle whose construction will be examined below.

Opinion (*iqnā' ẓanni*), in turn, is where there is *tarjīḥ* between the two possibilities, in other words, where one has a *taṣdīq* together with holding simultaneously the possibility or the suspicion of its opposite. The degrees of *taṣdīq* lead to the establishment of the various syllogisms and the type of judgements that they can deliver, and the type of definitions that correlate to conceptualizations. At the end of the *faṣl*, the author states that the goal of the treatise is to establish the ways to certain judgement and veridical conceptualization.[60]

Two key figures to examine are Ibn Sīnā and Fakhr al-Dīn al-Rāzī, especially as the latter's response to the former's encapsulation of the subject is key to Ibn Sīnā's admirers and antagonizers in the later *kalām* tradition. It is Rāzī's presentation and critical approach to Ibn Sīnā's epistemology that largely determines the course of the later tradition's treatment of metaphysical questions.

Primarily Ibn Sīnā states that metaphysics, *al-falsafa al-ūlā*, universal science, is ontology; in as far as its subject matter is existent qua existent, but also a theology, since it has as its goal the knowledge of God.[61] In the *Ilāhiyyāt*, he also sets out the interconnectedness of metaphysics with logic and the other theoretical and practical sciences, and more importantly how metaphysics establishes epistemological foundations for the other sciences.[62] This latter point establishes the dominance and pre-eminence of metaphysics over the other sciences.[63]

In terms of the hierarchy of the sciences, Ibn Sīnā states at the beginning of his *Ilāhiyyāt* that metaphysics as first philosophy validates or verifies the principles of the other sciences,[64] *wa-annahā tufīdu taṣḥīḥ mabādi' sā'ir al-'ulūm*. In *Ilāhiyyāt* I.2.14–15, he further stipulates that there is one part of metaphysics that investigates the principles (*mabādi'*) of the particular sciences as the principles of the more particularized science are to be sought in a higher science; for example, the principles of medicine being sought in the science of physics (*'ilm al-ṭabī'ī*). Since each science lower, or one should say more particularized or materialized, than metaphysics investigates the *aḥwāl* of particular existents, the principles of those sciences must be sought in the science that investigates the states of the existent (*aḥwāl al-mawjūd*), the *a'amm* (most general) of subject matters. Ibn Sīnā states '*fa-hādhā huwa al-'ilmu al-maṭlūb fī hādhihi al-ṣinā'a wa-huwa al-falsafa al-ūlā, li-annahu al-'ilm bi-awwal al-umūr fī al-wujūd, wa-huwa al-'illatu al-ūlā wa-awwal al-umūr fī al-'umūm, wa-huwa al-wujūd wa-l-waḥda*' ('Then this is the science sought after in this art, and it is first philosophy, because it is knowledge of the first thing in existence, and this is the first cause, and the first things in generality, and this is existence and unity').

Similarly, in *Burhān* II.7, Ibn Sīnā maintains that the particular sciences are not parts of metaphysics but are subordinated to it, but metaphysics itself is not subordinated to any other science. The principles (*mabādi'*), therefore, of all the other sciences are verified (*taṣiḥḥu*) or proven (*tubayy-anu*) in metaphysics (*al-falsafa al-ūlā*). He further states in the *Ilāhiyyāt*:

> We say that these [things] that are subject matters in other sciences become [proper] accidents in this science. For they are states that occur or inhere in 'existent' and are a division of it. Therefore, what is not demonstrated in another science is demonstrated here (*mā lā yubarhanu 'alayhi fī 'ilm ākhar yubarhanu 'alayhi hā hunā*).[65]

In *Burhān* II.7.165.3–7, Ibn Sīnā clarifies the commonality of the superior science of metaphysics when he states:

> As to that science whose commonality (*'umūmuhu*) is at the same level as the commonality of the existent and the one (*al-mawjūd wa-l-wāḥid*), it cannot be that a science about things below this commonality could be a part (*juz'an*) of the science of this commonality … and, indeed, it is necessary that the particular sciences are not part of this common science. Since the existent and the one are common to all subject matters (*li-jamī' al-mawjūdāt*), it is thus necessary that all other sciences are below this science which investigates [the existent and the one]; and as there is no subject matter more common than these two, it cannot be that the science investigating these two is below another science.

This essentially refers back to the fact that unlike a predicamental term that is restricted to a kind of existent, *mawjūd* is what may be termed transcendental, which applies to any class, category, or genus. In the first *faṣl* of the opening chapter of the *Burhān,* Ibn Sīnā introduces the two ways of knowledge, namely, *taṣawwur* and *taṣdīq*. So that the first principle of a subject matter is to be arrived at through either *taṣawurrāt* (conceptualizations) by way of real definitions (*ḥadd ḥaqīqī*) concerning the subject matter's essential attributes (*aʿrāḍ dhātiyya*), or *taṣdīqāt* (assents) arrived at by the syllogism (*qiyās*).[66]

> We say that every discipline – especially the theoretical one – has [i] principles, [ii] subject matters (*mawdūʿāt*), and [iii] questions (*masāʾil*). [i] Principles are the premises from which that discipline demonstrates, without them being demonstrated in that discipline either because they are evident, or because they are of too high a rank to be demonstrated in it, and are demonstrated only in a superior science, or because they are of too low a rank to be demonstrated in that science, but rather [they are demonstrated] in an inferior science (even though this is rare). [ii] Subject matters are the things of which the discipline investigates only (*innamā*) the states related to them, and the essential accidents belonging to them. [iii] Questions are the propositions whose predicates are the essential accidents of this subject matter, or of its species, or of its accidents; doubts arise about them, and hence their state is clarified in that science.
>
> Principles are the things from which the demonstrative proof is, questions are the things of which the demonstrative proof is, subject matters are the things about which the demonstrative proof is. It is as if the purpose of that about which the demonstrative proof is were the essential accidents, [the purpose of] that for the sake of which that [i.e. the demonstrative proof] is were the subject matter, and [the purpose of that] from which [the demonstrative proof is] were the principles.[67]

What are sought after in a science are its essential accidents, or we can say properties, *aʿrāḍ dhātiyya* (literally, the accidental characteristics). Only these can be properly under investigation in the respective science, since essential characteristics are naturally contained in the conceptualization (*taṣawwur*) of the *mawdūʿ*, and this *taṣawwur* must precede any investigation by necessity, as the latter is contingent upon it. The *aʿrāḍ dhātiyya* are the problems or questions (*masāʾil*) of the subject matter. They consequently form no part of the definition for the subject matter. They must be investigated, however, as they are by definition open to question or to demonstration, which in turn presupposes *mabādi'*, either as definitions or self-evident propositions (*qaḍāyā badīhiyya*), being the starting points, postulates, or ultimate premises. The starting points here are the premises (*muqaddimāt*) upon which the subject matter is logically dependent.

If the *mawjūd* (existent) is made the subject of the science of metaphysics, as we see in the *Ilāhiyyāt* I.2.14, then does that mean that the principles of existents cannot be investigated within the science? How, then, does metaphysics gain its principles as a science? Ibn Sīnā answers by his description of first philosophy as *aʿammu min al-ʿulūm al-juzʾiyya li-ʿumūm mawḍūʿihā* ('more common than the particular sciences due to the commonality of its subject matter'), and which takes its *mabādi'* from *al-muqaddimāt al-burhāniyya al-yaqīniyya* ('demonstrative and certain premises').[68]

In recapitulating, we can say that the ordering of the sciences requires a correct understanding of metaphysics, which is that knowledge that deals with those things that are the most immaterialized, and do not depend consequently on matter for their reality. This allows it a regulative function that other sciences do not have, since there is nothing more common than the notion of existence. It treats of that in things which is universally predicable of everything that is real. In terms of its relations with other sciences, the physicist, the chemist, and the biologist must adhere to it because by belonging to particular sciences, they examine and study only particular kinds of being, namely, a part of reality. A biologist deals with organic matter as part of the remit of his science, but he does not engage in questions regarding the meaning of life within that remit. He takes the reality of life for granted. Similarly, a physicist measuring an accelerating body, for example, takes the reality of motion for granted. The chemist equally so takes the reality of matter for granted. These sciences do not permit one to enter into the reality of things, as only metaphysics can. More importantly, when those scientists enter into those discourses, they do so as metaphysicians not as physicists, biologists, or chemists, and correspondingly what they say must be evaluated and judged on the basis of metaphysics and not of their particular sciences.

Al-ʿIlm al-Ḍarūrī or ʿNecessary Knowledge'

The Islamic intellectual tradition as a whole manifestly makes a critical distinction between necessary knowledge and acquired or deductive knowledge. Necessary knowledge, *in fine,* is the knowledge that imposes itself on the mind without any deductive process taking place. It is, furthermore, that knowledge which cannot be arrived at through any form of reasoning and demonstration.[69]

At the beginning of the *Madkhal* I.2, Ibn Sīnā states that the purpose of philosophy or conceptual thought is to arrive at the reality of things (*ḥaqāʾiq al-ashyāʾ*), in as far as it is possible for the human being to do so. However, in his later notebooks, he qualifies this assertion:

> It is not within the power of the human being to grasp the realities of things. Of things, we only know their properties, concomitants, and accidents. But we do not know the constitutive differentiae (*fuṣūl muqawwima*) for each one of them, indicating [that thing's] reality. We only know that they are things which have properties, accidents, and concomitants. We do not know the reality of the First [Being] (*al-Awwal*), the Intellect, the soul, the [heavenly] spheres, fire, air, water, and earth. Nor do we know [even] the reality of the accidents.[70]

Since all the sciences for Ibn Sīnā originate with the senses, the knowledge of things is based on a foundation of sensory experience, and thus man's ability to know only accidents. Therefore, what can be known by the intellect regarding things are their *lawāzim,* yielding a summary form of knowledge (*mujmalan*).[71] The implications of this will be discussed further below.

The degree of knowledge of things notwithstanding, the statement in the *Madkhal* implies that there is a necessary relationship between the order of mind and the order of individuated concrete existents in the external world. The relation must also be adequately sufficient to permit a relationship of knowledge, so that one may know in the mind that thing which exists out there in the external world with a degree of certainty. One of the definitions of truth (*al-ḥaqq*) found in the *Ilāhiyyāt* 1.8.48 is ʿthe state of the verbal statement or of the belief indicating the state of the external thing, if it corresponds to it (*muṭābiq lahu*), such that we would say, "This is a true statement" and "This is a true belief."ʾ

The speculative sciences all employ demonstrative syllogisms to arrive at the knowledge in their *masā'il*. The concepts embodied in their starting points or principles are so simple that the relations expressed between the concepts can be immediately apprehended by the mind without recourse to simpler terms or any middle terms.[72] All demonstrative knowledge thus is arrived at by a prior knowledge (*wa-kull taʿlīm wa-taʿallum dhihnī wa-fikrī yaḥṣulu bi-ʿilm qad sabaq*), which cannot be the product of demonstrations, or else it would amount to circularity (*dawr*).[73] If all knowledge can only come about on the basis of previous knowledge, logically so to speak, there must, then, be a notion of a first principle of *taṣawwur* and *taṣdīq*, a primary cognitive starting point that does not depend on previous learning.

Those fundamentals (*uṣūl*) that are to be known prior to any demonstration are the definitions (*ḥudūd*) of a science, postulates (*awḍāʿ*), and axioms or primitives (*muqaddimāt*). Definitions (*ḥudūd*) are those that provide the *taṣawwurāt* of the *mawḍūʿāt* and their accidentals that are not clearly conceptualized, hence their need to be demonstrated. Postulates are *muqaddimāt* that are not obvious in themselves, but a student proponent (*ṭālib*) concedes to accept them and their explanation. Axioms are self-evident (*bayyina bi-nafsihā*) principles of thought and thus cannot be denied by those held to be *compos mentis*, some principles being specific to a science and others being general.[74]

In *al-Jawhar al-naḍīd*, one of the many commentaries on Ṭūsī's *Tajrīd al-ʿaqāʾid*, by ʿAllāma Ḥillī, the commentator concisely sets out and explicates the position of the *mabādiʾ* in any science, basing himself, sometimes verbatim, on Ṭūsī's commentary on Ibn Sīnā's *Ishārāt*.[75] He states there that they are the foundations of principial knowledge. Principles can be either *taṣawwurāt* or *taṣdīqāt*. As *taṣawwurāt*, they are the definitions of things that are utilized in the particular science, either as the subject matter of a science (*mawḍūʿ al-ʿilm*), or as a part of the subject matter (*juzʾ min al-mawḍūʿ*), or as a derivative of the subject matter (*juzʾī taḥt al-mawḍūʿ*), or as an essential accident (*ʿaraḍ dhātī*). As *taṣdīqāt*, they are the primitives (*muqaddimāt*) on which the syllogisms are formed in any particular science.[76]

These latter principles take a propositional form that is either axiomatic (*awwaliyyāt*) or non-axiomatic. The former are propositions (*qaḍāyā*) that do not require any mediation or demonstration in order for them to be understood, and are known as the self-evident principles (*al-uṣūl al-*

muta'ārafa), which are absolute principles (*mabādi''alā al-iṭlāq*). Those that are non-axiomatic must be a priori accepted as postulates or hypotheses from other sciences wherein they may be demonstrated, but in any case, cannot be inferred or necessarily demonstrated from within the science in which they are being used. These are known as postulated principles (*uṣūl mawḍū'a*), in that when they are adopted on a working hypothetical basis, they are known more specifically as *muṣādarāt*, and when conceded in good faith (*ma'a al-musāmaḥa*) as postulates, then known as *awḍā'*.[77]

To clarify the above, we can state that there are two kinds of principles. First, in every particular science there is a set of fundamental constitutive principles that are proper to that science and recognized by it. Second, all the sciences have a set of common principles, including those by which the individual sciences are distinguished and interrelated. The first set of principles referred to is assumed by the investigator in that science and cannot be questioned by him in his role of investigator within that science. If he wishes to seek a demonstration of such principles, then this must be sought in a superior science. The second set of principles, first or common principles, are assumed by all the sciences and cannot consequently be directly demonstrated, not even by metaphysics. They can be subject to a negative demonstration by way of a *reductio ad absurdum* (*qiyās al-khulf*).[78] The latter consists in revealing that any proposition depends on the implicit or explicit assumption of the common principles without exception.

A few questions may present themselves at this point and should perhaps be examined. The first question, one can surmise, would surface from the notion of scientific reasoning. It was stated earlier that it was necessary for subordinate sciences to assume their fundamental principles and the existence of their subject matter from a higher science. The simple reason for this, aside from the hierarchical requirements exacted in the classificatory order, resides in the fact that the assent to, or rejection of, the truth of the principles is beyond the investigator's bounds within those sciences in which they are operating. If, on the other hand, they were not assumed, the investigator would then surely be left with facts alone, facts which in themselves are not sufficient to amount to a science. Were it not to be so, there would otherwise be no distinction of relation between the essential and the accidental when examining facts. Can the investigator, then, once having assumed the principles, subject them to a critical enquiry, that is to say, confirm or reject them? The simple answer, again unsurprisingly, is that they would not be able to do so. Any discussion of the principles would take them beyond the limit of their science. Any discussion of the principles is a discussion of the structural framework of the science in question, which would jeopardize its existence, as the justification of principles resides only within the science of metaphysics. If the principles are denied, then a science has nothing to say, and we are then left simply with facts. What is, then, the role of the investigator within a science? Their role is to restrict themselves to problems that arise from the framework erected by principles. One can also say that their main task is to demonstrate that the principles relate to the particular genus, which the science in question assumes.

As was elicited, every particular science adopts postulates, and assumptions, which are useful or necessary. These are not the product of scientific investigation, however, nor are they subject to verification in that science. What therefore are we to make of beliefs or theories held by contemporary natural scientists if we take this on board? We can say they are postulates or simple prejudicial premises. They cannot be conclusions of science, nor are they related to the structure of science. A prejudice, or hypothesis, is not necessarily untrue, but must always be uncritical. They can be said to be the result of the imposition of experience on the intellect. Everything brought about by experience, though, carries the proviso that it is the result of a limited experience. This should be kept in mind when commentators become lyrical in their treatment of science. Science is not a body of ascertained truth, a fact much forgotten by the adherents of scientism. This is because a scientific theory is never itself a fact, but the interpretation of facts in the light of a hypothesis. The substitution of scientific theory as a replacement for tenet in *'aqīda*, consequently, is a gross misunderstanding of scientific theory, not *'aqīda*. *Kalām* apologists, when confronting scientific fetishism, rarely note this. To establish a scientific theory as a religious tenet is to remove the scientific theory from the field of scientific investigation. The classification of the sciences outlined demonstrates that there is no singular uniform science, and thus no general conclusions of science as a whole. Any scientific conclusion, in order to be classified as scientific, must be one of the conclusions of a particular science or not at all.

One further point to be made at this juncture concerns the legitimacy of a superior science in the classificatory order to examine or justify the principles of a lower science. If there is a relation between the subordinate science and the superior science, for example, as was stated earlier between mathematics and harmonics, or geometry and optics, the principles of the subordinate, or more correctly here, subalternate, can be demonstrated in the superior science. If there is no relation between the subordinate and the superior sciences, then the science of metaphysics takes on the role of the examination of the principles of the subordinate science.

A few clarifications can be made here in view of the contemporary intellectual landscape. Any discussion of first principles must begin by using those same principles and not by their prior justification. An objection might, then, be made as to whether this procedure does not propose the demand of strict proofs, since it is ostensibly subjective and unscientific. It should be recognized at the outset that a proof in line with the objection to it must involve a second party as well as the proposer of a truth. Furthermore, a few other factors must be present before this truth can be proven to another. The first is that the proposer must be ready to fully assent to that truth, the second that the party examining the proof must be willing to be open to the truth, and finally that there be a means of communication that can adequately transmit the truth without distortion or unforeseen accretion. Psychological receptivity is of paramount concern here, as the second party must be willing to accept the proposed truth when demonstrated, and equally have the requisite intellectual aptitude to understand what is being demonstrated. Even if the first two factors are satisfactorily fulfilled, this leaves the third factor of communication. This involves the proficiency of the rules and meaning of language that is a prerequisite for the one conveying the proof as well as the listener. These observations will necessarily guide our analysis below of the principle of non-contradiction.

To reiterate, the *taqsīm* (division) of *'ilm* is in two categories, *badīhī* or *ḍarūrī* (self-evident or necessary/immediate) and *naẓarī* (theoretical). The *badīhī*, however, is not, strictly speaking, synonymous with the *ḍarūrī*, but is more specific, despite the overwhelming habit of the manualists in using the terms synonymously. Every *badīhī* is *ḍarūrī*, but not every *ḍarūrī* is *badīhī*. In a *taṣdīq badīhī*, for example, the two terms, subject and predicate, may both be the products of acquired knowledge; nevertheless, the intellectual conviction arises from the proposition simply when there is *taṣawwur* of both the subject and predicate, that is to say, they become known. This occurs without there being any logical reasoning or thought to connect the two. The *ḍarūrī*, by way of distinction, is that which is immediately known by a cause (*sabab*) such as the judgement that fire is hot, which is premised on touch (*lams*).[79]

In 'Aḍud al-Dīn al-'Ījī's *Mawāqif*, as in most other textbooks, the *'ulūm al-ḍarūriyya*, the necessary or immediate knowledges, are declared by Jurjānī to be the basis for all acquired knowledge (*al-'ulūm al-kasbiyya*), in that they are all reducible to them.[80] The absence of these, it is further stated, would nullify any search for knowledge, for they are the first principles (*al mabādi' al-ūlā*). The *ḍarūrī* class of knowledge is usually treated in three main categories, those that are arrived at by sensory perception, those that are arrived through inductive experience, and those that are axiomatic (such as the principle of non-contradiction and the principle of the excluded middle). These three categories, it should be remembered, demand no intellectual effort from us; they impose themselves on us in different ways. The sensory *ḍarūrī* knowledge imposes itself on us in conjunction with our sensory perceptions. The inductive *ḍarūrī* knowledge imposes itself on us through our observation of regularities in the natural order. The axiomatic *ḍarūrī* knowledge imposes itself on us by the *taṣawwur* of the two terms.

Al-Ījī divides the *ḍarūrī* into two main categories, the *wijdāniyyāt* and the category of *ḥissiyyāt* and *badīhiyyāt*. The *wijdāniyyāt* (usually identified as a subcategory of the *mushāhadāt*) are the feelings elicited by the internal senses, *al-ḥawāss al-bāṭina*, representing emotional perception such as sadness or joy. This type of knowledge is primary but is of little use, according to Ījī, as it does not cognitively benefit a third party who is not subject to this perception, and consequently cannot be used for demonstration. The other consolidating category is the *ḥissiyyāt*, which includes, according to Jurjānī, all knowledges that are derived from sense perception, or where sense perception is party to the acquisition of that knowledge. When we say derived, however, what is meant is that the grounds for *taṣdīq* are provided by the senses, but the *taṣdīq* itself can only be by way of *'aql*. According to Jurjānī, this category comprises, *inter alia*, the *maḥsūsāt* (the other subcategory of *mushāhadāt*), things perceived by the external senses, *al-ḥawāss al-ẓāhira*, such as the rain falling from the sky; the *tajrībiyyāt* (or sometimes referred to as the *mujarrabāt*), which are judgements arrived at by observation and experimentation, typically involving a disclosure of a causal connection as in medicine; and the *mutawātirāt*, transmitted knowledge, propositions that are based on a unanimous testimony of authorities representing the intellectual impossibility of collusion in a lie.

The last type of perception-based knowledge stated by Jurjānī is that arrived at by way of the *ḥadsiyyāt*, knowledge arrived at by strong intuition (*ḥads qawī*). In his commentary on this passage, Çelebi states that intuitively based knowledge is usually considered to be based on premises unrelated to sense perception, but he adds that the discussion here rather concerns specifically the *ḍarūriyyāt* in general and not intuition as specifically understood. The notion or general example given is that the moon receives its light from the sun, which is intuitively received partially by way of sense perception.[81] Siyalkoti reiterates in his commentary on the same passage that this intuition arises from repeated observations (*takrār al-mushāhada*) as declared by Ījī later on in the *Mawāqif* when discussing the premises for the syllogism.[82] The interesting point that naturally arises here is the question of how one can distinguish this type of intuitive knowledge from that acceded to as part of the *mujarrabāt*. The judgements of the latter are arrived at through repeated observations of a process, which in turn help to elicit the discovery of a hidden syllogism. The judgements of the *ḥadsiyyāt* are the knowledge arrived at by a repeated observation of a process by eliciting the cause as well as the knowledge of the essence of the cause (*maʿlūm bi-l-māhiyya*).[83] Çelebi further states in his commentary that, strictly speaking, repeated observations are not required for *ḥadsiyyāt* as in *mujarrabāt*, but a further distinction between the two can be made through the latter's requirement of repeated multiple observations for the eliciting of the hidden syllogism, whereas for the former, if needed at all, comprise one or two incidents of observation.[84]

The *ʿilm al-badīhī* is one that does not require reasoning in order for it to be attained. As to *ʿilm al-naẓarī*, the knowledge is acceded to through deliberation or meditation (so in effect acquired, *kasbī*). Each type is further divided into *taṣawwur badīhī* (self-evident conceptualization that is intuitively perceived, such as *wujūd* or *shayʾ*, 'thing') and *taṣawwur naẓarī* (for example, a *ḥadd* or *rasm,* or conception of the reality of the angels), and *taṣdīq badīhī* (judgement of self-evidence, 'the whole is greater than the part') and *taṣdīq naẓarī* (theoretical judgement, 'the world is temporally originated').[85] An acquired judgement (*taṣdīq naẓarī*), therefore, is obtained through demonstration, whilst a self-evident judgement (*taṣdīq badīhī*), which by definition cannot be demonstrated, is grasped due to its axiomatic self-evidence. It is quite simply that which once presented to the mind is undeniable. The *taṣdīq naẓarī* is dependent on the *taṣdīq badīhī*, in that the latter is utilized to arrive at the former by way of the syllogisms, and correspondingly the *taṣawwur naẓarī* is dependent on the *taṣawwur badīhī*, in that the latter is utilized to arrive at the former by way of definition.

The Epistemological Dimension

The A Priori Form of Knowledge

In the realm of self-evident simple apprehension or conception (*taṣawwur*), the *taṣawwur awwali*, such as the notion of *wujūd* (existence), is the first intellection of being or reality, that which is in actuality. The *umūr ʿāmma* (general matters) chapters of the central post-Rāzian *kalām* treatises more often than not begin with the examination of this most self-evident conception (*taṣawwur*) as the first *masʾala*. It is well to note that the discussions that arise in relation to the self-evidence of *wujūd* do not present any contradiction. The relevance of this question lies in that it enables us to examine the extent to which realities that impose themselves upon us as self-evident, or a priori concepts, can be discussed and demonstrated, and if so, the specific nature of the issue pertaining to them that may be demonstrated.

It is true that if *wujūd* is self-evident, then a discourse pertaining to establishing that quality may be considered a contradiction in point. The examination of this question, though, avoids this charge by addressing the self-evidence of the concept of self-evidence and not the concept itself. When Ījī, in the *Mawāqif*, states that the self-evidence of *taṣawwur* is a *ṣifa* (attribute or quality) that is extraneous to it, Jurjānī comments in corroboration that 'this extraneous quality may be sought by way of demonstration (*burhān*).'[86] Siyalkoti adds in another part of his commentary on Ījī relating to the self-evidence of *ʿilm* that the *ḥukm* of the self-evidence of the self-evident (*badāhat al-badīhī*) may be a speculative question due to the heedlessness of some who might require reminding. This shows that sometimes a demonstration may be necessary to show the connection or identity between the predicate and subject, the proposition being mediately self-evident. Çelebi in his super-commentary on the same passage seals the argument by helpfully stating that the self-evidence of the knowledge of something does not entail the self-evident knowledge of its self-evidence, and thus the proof of its self-evidence can be sought (*badāhat al-'ilm bi-shay' lā tastalzim al-'ilm al-badīhī bi-badāhatihi wa-lidhā yustadall 'alayhā*).[87]

The most self-evident of concepts, as cited above, is *wujūd*, whose self-evidence is set out in three ways by Rāzī in his *Mulakhkhaṣ fī al-ḥikma wa-l-manṭiq*,[88] in a section examining the self-evident nature of the *taṣawwur* of *wujūd*. These are rehearsed, examined, and debated for the most part and in varying degrees by subsequent authors, such as Bayḍāwī,[89] Ṭūsī,[90] and Kātibī,[91] and notably commented on by Iṣfahānī,[92] Ḥillī,[93] and others. In his commentary on Ṭūsī's *Tajrīd al-'aqā'id*, Iṣfahānī follows Ṭūsī in reciting two out of the three ways.[94] This provides a useful instance of the said literature.

Iṣfahānī begins by citing that the first way states[95] that the concept of *wujūd* is self-evident, because the self-evident *taṣdīq* is by way of mutual exclusion (*al-tanāfī*), the mutual exclusion of the proposition and its contradiction, its truth or falsehood. So that in the statement 'Either a thing exists (*al-shay' immā an yakūna mawjūdan*) or does not exist (*ma'dūman*),' the proposition is contingent on the *taṣawwur* of *wujūd* and *'adam*. This is an ontological question, one should readily notice, rather than simply a logical question, and thus a metaphysical enquiry first and foremost with logical implications. Logical laws will not thus enter constitutively into the answer but will marshal the evidence for it. What is meant in this instance is that everyone of sound mind recognizes the contradiction of simultaneously conjoining existence and non-existence. This judgement is contingent on the conception of existence and non-existence. It follows therefore that that which the self-evident is contingent upon must also be self-evident, and thus the *taṣawwur* of *wujūd* and that of *'adam* are *badīhī*.

The second way states that the *taṣawwur* of *wujūd* is self-evident, as established above, because we have that conception. Further, this conception is either through self-evidence (*badāha*) or by way of acquired knowledge (*kasb*), and since there is no intermediary between the two, and the way of *kasb* is impossible (*mumtani'*), *wujūd* is *badīhī*.[96] Iṣfahānī comments that this is so because were the conception to be arrived at by *kasb*, then either it is known by way of itself, so that it is contingent upon itself, or by way of its parts. If these parts are concrete existents (*wujūdāt*), then it follows that *wujūd* is contingent on itself, and its definition will be also contingent on itself, which is absurd. Furthermore, if the *taṣawwur* of *wujūd* were arrived at through *kasb*, then it would have to be arrived at by way of definition (*ḥadd*) or description (*rasm*). This would consequently be false because definition is composed of genus (*jins*) and differentia (*faṣl*), and *wujūd* has neither genus nor differentia. In the case of *rasm*, which is composed of the proximate genus (*jins qarīb*) and a particular accident (*ʿaraḍ khāṣṣ*), the possibility is rejected for the same reason, in that we can inductively ascertain that *wujūd* is more general and known than anything that might be used for its description.

This can be explained perhaps a little more clearly. The definition of *wujūd* cannot be arrived at by tautology or else it would constitute a circular argument (*dawr*). Neither can the conception of existence be arrived at through its parts, since if these parts constituted existents, it would amount to the same problem. If the parts are not existents, then one would have to accept their existence had come about by way of their cumulative aggregation, and thus as an accident of this. This would further make their coming together the cause of their existence, rather than holding them to be parts of existence.

The above discussions go to the heart of the matter relating to the constitutive parts of the conceptual structure of the self-evident propositions, such as the principle of non-contradiction, which require a *taṣawwur* of both parts of the proposition. This is, namely, whether the parts constituting the proposition in question require demonstration and thus taint the self-evidence of the whole, or whether they enjoy necessarily the status of the whole. The discussion is important because what is at issue throughout this paper is how one can arrive at a formal beginning in terms of principle, and specifically with the primacy of the principle of non-contradiction as a self-evident proposition.

To reiterate, then, the self-evident *badīhī* proposition cannot be demonstrated because direct proof of an intuitive truth is not possible. By a direct proof we mean where the relation between subject and predicate is so immediate that no middle term is necessary, because the meaning of the predicate is contained in that of the subject. First principles (*uṣūl mutaʿārafa, awwaliyāt*) are principles of natural intelligence, or what may be termed our natural reason that we all possess, *ḍarūrī* knowledge, and can either be *taṣawwurāt badīhiyya* or *taṣdīqāt badīhiyya*. They are the pillars of all *ḍarūrī* knowledge that cannot be negated or doubted by the sane mind.

When we perceive intelligible reality, the first principles are those self-evident principles that arise in us from the intuitive grasp of this reality. When we say reality, we are naturally referring here to existence (*wujūd*) as the fundamental and principal self-evident idea in the realm of *taṣawwur*. The immediate *lawāzim* (*consequentae*) of this idea furnish us with the first principles as ontological realities. Intuition (*ḥads*) is described typically in the commentary of the *Shamsiyya* (following Ibn Sīnā's *Burhān*), as the immediate movement of the mind from principle to comprehension,[97] whereas ordinary thought (*fikr*) is the movement of the mind to the principle first, and then back to the object sought (*maṭlūb*). In actuality there is no movement that takes place in intuition, as the mere figuring of the principle in the mind brings forth the result through the spontaneous apprehension of the middle term.[98] This apprehension is a gift whose source is a *fayḍ ilāhī* (divine effusion or effulgence), according to Ibn Sīnā.[99] This is the highest form of intuition known as *al-ḥads al-qudsī* (sanctified intuition), similar to that given to the prophets ﷺ but upon a differing degree.

In order to situate the above better, a discussion of the cognitive processes involved would better position the role of the *awwaliyyāt*. Fakhr al-Dīn al-Rāzī, following Ibn Sīnā and al-Kindī, depicts the human intellect in the form of a quadripartite division. The four stages of the intellect can perhaps be better understood as four relations that the intellect possesses vis-à-vis intelligibles. The first stage or faculty in order is the material intellect (*al-ʿaql al-hayūlānī*), then the dispositional intellect, *intellectus in habitu* (*al-ʿaql bi-l-malaka*), then the actual intellect (*al-ʿaql bi-l-fiʿl*), and then the acquired intellect (*al-ʿaql al-mustafād*). The material intellect requires an external agent to actualize it, and is thus dormant, potential, until it is activated by an intelligible (*maʿqūl*). The dispositional intellect becomes actualized when the primary intelligibles (*maʿqūlāt ūlā*) and axioms (*mabādiʾ ʿāmma*) have been fully assimilated. These are the foundations that are necessary for the *ʿulūm al-naẓariyya*, the theoretical sciences. These latter are acquired by the actual intellect.[100]

Following Ibn Sīnā, Rāzī explains that the acquisition of knowledge by the *ʿaql bi-l-malaka* can occur in two ways. The first is through *ṭalab* and *fikr*, study and cogitation, and the second by way of *ḥads* intuition. The difference between the two is important to grasp, the first can be deductive and inductive, and the latter is either extensive or limited, encompassing knowledge of whole sciences or merely the middle terms. The highest form of *hads* is called *al-quwwa al-qudsiyya* or *al-nafs al-qudsiyya*.[101] This faculty is associated with *al-'aql bi-l-malaka* and *al-'aql bi-l-fi'l*, precisely the two that are concerned with primary knowledge and its transition to syllogistic knowledge. Rāzī, however, limits the faculty to *al-'aql bi-l-malaka* in contradistinction to Ibn Sīnā and Ghazālī.[102] In the *Ishārāt*, Ibn Sīnā states the difference between *fikr* and *hads* in the following way:

> Thought is a certain movement of the soul among concepts. For the most part, it is assisted by the imagination (*al-takhayyul*). By means of it the soul seeks the middle term (*al-hadd al-awsaṭ*), or what resembles it, of whatever leads to knowledge of the unknown in the case of the absence [of such knowledge]. This is done in the manner of disclosing that which is concealed internally or the like. Sometimes thought leads to the conclusion sought (*al-maṭlūb*) and sometimes it is disrupted. As for intuition, it presents the middle term in the mind at once, either after search and desire without movement (*haraka*) or without desire (*min ghayr ishtiyāq*) and movement. Its intermediate, or what is of the same order, is also represented with it.[103]

In his commentary on this passage, Rāzī states that *hads* and *fikr* share a similarity in one aspect and differ in another. They both have in common a *haraka* that occurs in the mind (*dhihn*) going from the *hadd al-awsaṭ* to the *maṭlūb*. Their difference lies in that in *fikr*, the *maṭlūb* is first posited (*yūwḍa' al-maṭlūb awwalan*), and then the *hadd al-awsaṭ* that results in the *maṭlūb* is investigated. If the investigator (*ṭālib*) discovers the *hadd al-awsaṭ*, and is led to the *maṭlūb* by it, then his *fikr* has been successful; and correspondingly unsuccessful if such a term is not found. In the case of intuition, Rāzī as commentator states that the *hadd al-awsaṭ* is present first in the mind, leading the investigator from the term to the *maṭlūb*. This may occur, we are told, without there being any solicitation to obtain the *hadd al-awsaṭ*, in which case the awareness (*shu'ūr*) of the *hadd al-awsaṭ* precedes the *maṭlūb*. If there is a desire, on the other hand, to obtain the *hadd al-awsaṭ*, then the awareness of it is posterior to the awareness of the *maṭlūb*. In this scenario, he suggests that the awareness of the middle term in the mind closely follows the desire for it, albeit posterior to the awareness of the thing sought. In *fikr*, the sequence may be significantly longer.

It is well to notice that what is at issue here is the speed at which the mind achieves the object sought, rendering intuition, much like Aristotle's quick wit, of the same type of knowledge as reflexive thought, the difference being the rapidity by which the mind is made to operate. Although Rāzī admits to differing levels of, or propensities for, intuition, the highest being *al-quwwa al-qudsiyya,* he concludes that the qualitative difference of the person who possesses this heightened faculty is still one of speed.[104] This speed is the movement of the mind from first principles to secondary principles and from premises to conclusions. The nature of the knowledge, more properly syllogistic knowledge, as the result of ordinary thought remains nevertheless the same.

To contextualize the above, it is beneficial to set out concisely the levels of apprehension and the role of the internal powers of the human being according to Ibn Sīnā's *Ishārāt,* a classification that is mostly followed by the later tradition. Primarily the soul is the form of the body, which manages it. This substance is declared to be one and is the source of one's identity.[105] Ibn Sīnā establishes differing levels of apprehension (*idrāk*) depending on the faculty of apprehension, and the degree of abstraction (*tajrīd*) denoting the level of apprehension.

There are three types of apprehension, the notion of apprehension defined by Ibn Sīnā in the following way: 'To perceive a thing is to have its quiddity represented (*mutamaththila*) in the perceiver, by which the thing is perceived in him [i.e. the knower intuitively perceiving it].'[106] The first level of apprehension is that of the senses where one comes into contact with the object of apprehension and there is no degree of abstraction, as the object is apprehended unshorn of the accidents that envelop its quiddity. The second is when the object apprehended by the senses is no longer present to the senses, but can still be imagined, so that its form is represented internally. This is a weak form of abstraction as the internal imagination (*al-khayāl al-bāṭin*) imagines the thing with its accidents and cannot fully abstract the quiddity from them, but does abstract it sufficiently to be able to recall the thing when absent from the external senses.[107] The third level of apprehension is that of the abstraction of the quiddity by the intellect (*al-ʿaql*) making it fully intelligible.

The internal senses (*al-ḥawās al-bāṭina* or *al-mudrikāt al-bāṭiniyya*)[108] are to be found in the animal soul and are five in number, starting with common sense (*al-ḥiss al-mushtarak*), by which the *mudrikāt* from the external five senses are assembled, a faculty also that serves as the interface between the external and internal senses. Following this is the sensible memory or imagination (*al-quwwa al-muṣawwira* or *al-khayāl*), the depository of forms for the common sense, when the latter is absent, and therefore has a retentive rather than compositive role. The forms deposited in the *khayāl* are those arising from the experience of sensible perceptions. They are images waiting to be recollected by the intellect or internal faculties. The imaginative faculty is very powerful in that it can focus or distract the human soul, especially in its compositive form as *al-quwwa al-mutakhayyila*.

The sensible memory in the human soul when used by reason becomes the power of cognition (*al-quwwa al-mufakkira* or *al-fikr*). When the estimative faculty uses the sensible memory, it is known as imagination, *al-quwwa al-mutakhayyila*, which utilizes the depository of the forms of the common sense and estimative faculties and has the power to perceive, retain, compose, and divide forms (*ṣuwar*). This *quwwa mutakhayyila* is the faculty that represents the most subversive danger, according to Suhrawardī, as to its effects on the human soul.[109] Ibn Sīnā describes it as being in incessant activity, regardless of whether it is directed by *wahm* or *'aql*, dividing and composing images and forms at will or respectively under direction, but never still.

> Part of the nature of this imaginative faculty is to be continually preoccupied with the two storehouses of the formative and memorative [faculties], and to be always inspecting the forms, beginning from a sensed or remembered form, and transferring from it to a contrary or a similar [form], or to something which comes from it through a cause – for this is its nature.[110]

The fourth faculty is the estimative faculty (*al-wahm* or *al-quwwa al-wahmiyya*),[111] the ruling faculty in animals, which abstracts from individual sensible objects, such as the image of the wolf when perceived by sheep, in other words non-sensible meanings, so as to instigate flight from an impending danger. It is in effect what is understood as instinct. The last and fifth faculty is memory (*al-quwwa al-ḥāfiẓa al-dhākira*), which is the depository of the forms of the estimative faculty. The latter forms are *ma'ānī*, or intentions, which are to be distinguished from forms (*ṣuwar*). The *ma'nā* is the proper object of the faculty of estimation and refers to that which is non-sensible, but which is nevertheless without the mediation of the external senses.[112]

> The difference between the perception of the form (*idrāk al-ṣūra*) and the perception of the intention (*idrāk al-maʿnā*) is that the form is the thing that the internal sense (*al-ḥiss al-bāṭin*) and the external sense (*al-ḥiss al-ẓāhir*) perceive together, but the external sense perceives it first and presents it to the internal sense. For example, in the perception of the form of a wolf by a sheep, the latter perceives its form, that is to say, its shape, aspect, and colour, and for certain the internal sense of the sheep perceives these, but indubitably its external sense perceives them first. As to intention, it is that which the soul perceives from sensibilia (*al-ḥiss*) without previously having been perceived by the external sense. For example, the sheep's perception of the intention of the wolf's hostility or an intention that makes its fear of it necessary and its consequent flight, which the sense does not perceive. Now, what the external sense before anything perceives of the wolf, and which in turn is perceived by the internal sense, is properly designated in this context by the term 'form', and what the internal faculties perceive without the external sense is properly designated in this context by the term 'intention'.[113]

The common sense therefore collects all the sensations of the external senses, whilst each of the senses is limited to one type of perception. In that context, the common sense has powers of discrimination between each of the perceptions of the senses, but nevertheless possesses the capacity to determine that the differing qualities perceived pertain to the same object. Our consciousness, sense consciousness as distinguished from intellectual consciousness, comes from this faculty, which provides us with knowledge of ourselves, and also our experience of facts, without, however, offering any explanation of the facts. It can still be thought of as a reliable source of knowledge, albeit limited. It cannot, however, retain the forms itself but leaves this to the faculty of imagination (*al-khayāl*) as stated above. The faculty of imagination, sensible memory, prepares the ground for intellectual cognition. The estimative faculty uses this storehouse to evoke memories and to recall past perceptions and is able to make judgements of the imagination.[114]

The doors of cognitive perception of the form of an object are of four types of abstraction according to *Kitāb al-nafs*,[115] which operate together simultaneously so that one can say that there is always a unified psychic activity that is operative in the human or animal. Each faculty in this scheme functions in accordance with its capacity.

The first 'cognition' is that pertaining to the common sense (*al-ḥiss al-mushtarak*) in reliance on the external senses. This in effect is the first abstraction, so to speak. The various perceptions must be organized in a way that the differing perceptions are brought together by a faculty, and since animals are able to have this faculty, Ibn Sīnā argues that the intellect cannot be the faculty for this, hence the necessity of the faculty of common sense.[116] Ibn Sīnā explains that all perception is in one sense (*bi-naḥw min al-anḥā'*) a seizure of the form of that which is perceived (*akhdh ṣūrat al-mudrak*), in other words, an abstraction.[117] If that which is perceived is a material thing, then the form is abstracted from its materiality (*mujarrada 'an al-mādda tajrīdan*). When the common sense seizes this form, the form is seized together with the accidental attributes (*lawāḥiqihā al-'āriḍa*) of the material thing, and this seizure is in relation with the matter itself (*ma'a wuqū' al-nisba baynahā wa-bayn al-mādda*).[118] What this means is that if the relation (*nisba*) ceases, then the abstraction fails, because the sense imperfectly abstracts the form from matter, and thus has need of the existence of materiality so that the form may continue to present itself, or else it would disappear. This degree of perception therefore is tied to the material realm and is dependent upon it. The common sense here has also a power of synthesizing qualities that obtain in a material thing.

The second level of abstraction is that of the imagination, which is superior to that of the common sense, as it does not require the presence of the material object to remain present to the senses. The form can remain stored, to be brought to the fore when needed, but this form is an image that is not separate from the form. These images are also conserved together with their qualitative relations that they obtained in the world, and not simply as atomized forms.

The third level of abstraction is that of the estimative faculty (*al-wahm*), which is superior to that of the imagination, in that it can attain the intentions in its abstraction, which are in themselves immaterial, such as that which is suitable or harmful in a thing, but accidentally present in the material thing.[119] These intentions are not contained in the forms, but are complementary to the forms. It is the estimative faculty that comes closest to the intellect and is the reigning faculty for animals, allowing them to stay alive, feed themselves, and flee from danger by way of instinctive reactions (*ilhāmāt*). The fourth type of abstraction is that of the intellect, which concerns us the most and which we will examine once we have established the role of the third and fourth levels of the intellect for Ibn Sīnā and Rāzī.

As stated above, before dealing with the internal and external senses present in the animal soul, the knowledge of the first principles, the *awwaliyyāt,* takes place in *al-ʿaql bi-l-malaka.* This is the stage of the intellect where primary intelligibles come about in the material intellect. It is well to re-emphasize that Ibn Sīnā rejects the doctrine of innate ideas, since the material intellect (*al-ʿaql al-hayūlānī*) is primarily a *tabula rasa*, in that it is entirely potential. By way of these primary intelligibles (*maʿqūlāt ūlā*), further secondary intelligibles (*maʿqūlāt thāniya*) may, then, be acquired by way of syllogism.[120] These primary intelligibles are described specifically as premises of judgements (*muqaddimāt allatī yaqaʿ bi-hā al-taṣdīq*). We are told that they arise in the dispositional intellect, but how, it may be asked, does this take place? The building blocks or elements of the primary intelligibles according to Ibn Sīnā come from sense perception; it is the articulate soul (*al-nafs al-nāṭiqa*)[121] in its *fiṭrī* or *jibillī* mode of operation that processes them into propositions. The articulate soul in its speculative aspect, one must understand, is the intellect expressed in a quadripartite form in relation to the intelligibles; in other words, it possesses these four dispositions. Suhrawardī states that the movement from one disposition to another is due to the active intelligence.[122]

Once the primary axiomatic premises or self-evident (*badīhī*) universal concepts are acquired in the dispositional intellect, then it becomes disposed to acquire secondary intelligibles by way of the syllogism, as these concepts are the premises of syllogisms, or alternately by way of intuition. The third level of intellect, *al-ʿaql bi-l-fiʿl,* the actual intellect, is where the relation of the intellect to intelligibles is one where the acquired intelligibles can be called to the presence of the mind when desired, but the intellect is not presently thinking them; in other words, it has the potential to think them. The last relation of the intellect is that of the acquired intellect, *al-ʿaql al-mustafād,* where the intellect can call the intelligibles into its presence and is actually thinking them.

It should be pointed out that the intellect is a faculty higher and subtler than the senses, as it is free from the limitations of singularity and concreteness. Since the nature of a faculty defines the function of the faculty, on the basis that the function may be correctly said to follow essence, it means that the faculty is free from the materiality to which the senses are bound. The nature of the faculty must therefore be supramaterial and not part of the body, but rather dependent on the body. If it is a supra-material faculty, then it must belong to the soul, since it is not organic but can be termed anorganic. The brain, being a bodily organ, is the seat of the internal senses as per Ibn Sīnā and has a central part to play in regard to the external senses, but it cannot, then, be considered the seat of the intellect.

The syllogism yields conclusions by way of the discovery of the middle term that is common to the two premises of the syllogism. These conclusions express the intelligibles. The middle terms as intelligibles cannot be stored in the mind according to Ibn Sīnā and hence must be obtained from the Active Intellect (*al-ʿaql al-faʿʿāl*) each time they are sought. The discovery of the middle term, from our human perspective, may be found through the agency of intuition (*ḥads*) as stated earlier. The role of logical thinking therefore is to prepare the intellect to receive the middle term by way of intuition. At the highest level, this intuitional capacity is essentially the imprinting of the human intellect with the intelligibles in the Active Intellect.[123]

Knowledge of Self-evident Universal Propositions

First principles are *taṣdīqāt*, judgements that are first in the logical order. They are divided into two types, the first being common principles (*mabādiʾ ʿāmma*), and the second, proper principles (*mabādiʾ khāṣṣa*). The common principles are what are habitually termed the laws of thought, the principle of non-contradiction, the principle of the excluded middle, the principle of identity, and are our main interest here. They are either explicit (*bi-l-fiʿl*) in their application or implicit (*bi-l-quwwa*). The proper principles are those that pertain to the sciences, respectively, and are of three types. They are: judgements that are immediately evident propositions; judgements that are demonstrable propositions, assumed without demonstration; and lastly, concepts such as definitions.[124]

The assent to first principles is necessary, a point that is illustrated by Ibn Sīnā, for example, stating that it can only be rejected by the sophist, who knows it is true but chooses to deny it; the perplexed, who is someone who is intellectually challenged, so admits them without recognizing the fact, and the obdurate (*mu'ānid*), whose obstinacy flies in the face of even his own experience. The latter is a particularly difficult case, happily solved by Ibn Sīnā in a somewhat practical way. Those that adhere to a philosophy that does not admit first principles are difficult cases and cannot be directly refuted, since there can be no prior proposition in knowledge from which an inference may be made. Indirect refutation by way of retortion might properly offer the only effective methodology.[125]

In terms of propositions that are deemed necessary and axiomatic, Ibn Sīnā sets out in the *Burhān*, but also in the *Ishārāt*, those whose assent is by way of necessity (*taṣdīq 'alā wajh al-ḍarūra*). The *ḍarūra* here is either external (*ẓāhiriyya*), that is to say, by way of sense perception (*ḥiss*) or experiment (*tajriba*) or unanimous testimony (*tawātur*),[126] or internal (*bāṭiniyya*), by way of the intellect or through another internal faculty, such as the estimative faculty.[127] Those propositions that are *ḍarūrī* due to an internal necessity comprise the propositions that interest us here, namely, the *awwaliyyāt* that the pure intellect (*mujarrad al-'aql*) imposes on us, and propositions that contain their own syllogisms (*muqaddimāt fiṭriyya al-qiyās* or *qadāyā qiyasātuhā ma'ahā*). The *awwaliyyāt* consist of things such as Euclid's fifth axiom, 'the whole is greater than the part.' These are deemed to have internal necessity and rely entirely on the pure intellect. The mere *taṣawwur* of the terms in the proposition is sufficient to ensure *taṣdīq*. The intellect here sees the relation of the two ideas, 'whole' and 'part', to be such that the judgement is seen to be necessary. The truth of the judgement is seen to be true as an existing objective relation that is present, a relation between subject and predicate to which the intellect does not add nor contribute. The psychological element here naturally intrudes in the correct conceptualization of the terms, though, which may be clear to some and obscure for others.

They can also be propositions that provide within them their own syllogisms (*qadāyā qiyāsātuhā ma'ahā*), such as 'four is even', where the intellect has some support, instinctive support that is not external, from the intelligible, 'being divisible by two', as soon as the proposition 'four is even' is encountered. They can also be propositions that require the aid of one of the internal faculties of the soul, such as the estimative faculty, to acquire simple concepts to be used by the intellect.[128] If the support is instinctive, then it is considered *fiṭrī*, the notion of *fiṭra* being:[129]

> The meaning of *fiṭra* is [as follows]: if one imagines (*yatawahham*) himself as if he came to this world at once mature and wise (*bāligh ʿāqil*), except that he has never heard an opinion, never believed in any doctrine, nor was ever associated with a religious community, nor knew any political system, but has experienced (*shahida*) the objects of sense (*al-maḥsūsāt*) and abstracted from them sensible forms (*khayāliyyāt*). Then he submits something from among them to his mind and raises a doubt about it. If he is able to doubt it, then his *fiṭra* does not attest to it; but if he is not able to doubt it, then it is something which his *fiṭra* imposes upon him. But not everything that the *fiṭra* imposes upon the human being is true, but in fact much of it is false. Only the *fiṭra* of the faculty called intellect is true ... [sometimes the *fiṭra* of estimation makes wrong judgements] and it is known that this *fiṭra* is false and the reason for it is that this is the natural operation of a faculty (*jibillat quwwa*) that conceptualizes things only as objects of sensation (*ʿalā naḥw al-maḥsūs*).

Estimations (*wahmiyyāt*) are opinions or beliefs that are necessitated by the faculty of estimation (*quwwat al-wahm*), which in turn is dependent on the senses and passes judgements on sense objects.[130] These judgements are sometimes true and are acceded to by the intellect, but many are untrue. If the estimations are found to be untrue by the intellect, they nevertheless persist in the *khayāl*. This sometimes leads them to be indistinguishable from the *awwaliyyāt*, which are properly within the sphere of the intellect. The *fiṭra* of the faculty of estimation is an instrument of the intellect only insofar as it concerns the sensibles. In respect to non-sensible things, and due to its bias towards the sensibles, Ibn Sīnā considers it a false *fiṭra*.[131]

The Principle of Non-contradiction

It was stated that first principles are logical laws of reason, but we also further contend that they reflect ontological laws of reality. If it were not so, then we can say that the logically absurd, that which cannot be thought, could nevertheless exist. Whether the absurd is merely unthinkable or also unrealizable *in rerum natura* (*fī al-khārij*), namely, impossible ontologically, is what we intend to examine. If logical and ontological orders were distinct, it would mean that a squared circle, that which is inconceivable as a logical instance, could nevertheless be realizable in the real world. But we know that to be an impossible absurdity, so can the two orders be separable? We can state the logical form of the principle 'one cannot affirm and deny the same attribute in regard to the same thing in the same relation,' and restate it by way of an ontological counterpart, 'the same thing cannot be and not be at the same time.'

The conclusion we arrive at is that an absurdity cannot be conceived, and neither can it exist. This needs to be qualified somewhat so that it is more exacting. Some absurdities may be conceived in some form, it may be objected, which is true, but they can never amount to genuine concepts (*mafāhīm haqīqiyya*). The logically absurd, for example the squared circle (*dā'ira murraba'a*) mentioned above, can exist as a notion in the mind, but not being a real essence, it cannot exist in extramental reality. This latter impossibility is therefore conceivable in some sense in the mind, but nevertheless remains impossible extramentally. On the other hand, this can be distinguished from those things that may be non-existent, for example a unicorn, but nonetheless have logical existence. It does not follow, though, that its non-existence *de re* implies its impossibility, since its logical existence means it has an essence. The difference is that the squared circle has mental presence as a self-contradictory notion, that is to say, the mind can have *tasawwur* of it, but it does not possess real logical existence *per se*, and consequently has no essence. Having no essence, it cannot exist in extramental reality and is consequently impossible.

The time element in the principle of non-contradiction (PNC), the basis of a critical misunderstanding by Kant,[132] here refers to a simultaneous formal relation and not to a particularized instance of time, as naturally the principle is beyond time, as concurred with by the Königsberg philosopher. The time aspect refers to the impossibility of contradictory attributes inhering in the subject at the same instance, thus as a formal relation. This is also the manner in which one must understand Ibn Sīnā's reference to time in his formulation of opposition.

Although it is not intended in this section to provide a thorough treatment of opposition, it is nevertheless important to provide some guidelines as to the different types of oppositions in the Avicennan logical tradition which are pertinent to our purposes, and which will be examined further in the context of the square of opposition below. In *Kitāb al-maqūlāt,* Ibn Sīnā's commentary on Aristotle's *Categories,* he provides us with an effective definition of opposition:

> We say: opposites (*al-mutaqābilayn*) are those which do not unite (*lā yajtami'ān*) in one subject (*mawdū' wāḥid*) from one aspect (*jiha wāḥida*) in one time together (*fī zaman wāḥid ma'an*).[133]

The first opposition in importance, for our purposes, is the opposition of contradiction. This is undoubtedly the strictest form of opposition (*taḍādd*), a negative opposition, arising when there is opposition between an affirmation and its pure denial, but always reducible to the opposition between being and non-being. Whenever one of the opposites can be predicated of a subject, the other must be denied. They are mutual opposites that are not combined together in a single subject.[134] The second type of negative opposition, according to Ibn Sīnā, and following from Aristotle's *Categories,* is the opposition related to privation (*'adam*), where the one opposite expresses a perfection and the other a lack; for example, sightedness and blindness.[135] The relationship of the latter members of the pair is that of privation, so that blindness can only be said of a subject who could have been sighted, but sightedness is not predicated of them. Whereas contradiction presents us with a pure denial of the opposite, privation presents us with a denial of an opposite together with an expression of the absence of that opposite that could be predicated of the subject. Contraries, in contrast, are a case of positive opposition, in the sense they are an expression of positive extremes in a given genus. They can either admit a mediate position as between the two contraries, white and black, namely, grey, neither quite white nor quite black, or not, such as the contraries, odd and even, where no intermediary concept is admissible. The contrary goes further than contradiction, though, as it constitutes a denial of its opposite, as in contradiction, but also provides an affirmation of the positive extreme of its opposite.

Once the above context has been unfurled, we will turn to examine the *taṣdīqāt al-ḍarūriyya,* according to Rāzī in his *Muḥaṣṣal,*[136] which is also paraphrased by 'Aḍud al-Dīn Ījī in his *Mawāqif.* The said *taṣdīqāt* are divided into three types. The first are those that concern *ḥissiyyāt*, sensual perceptions (i.e. fire is hot); the second are *wijdāniyyāt*, internal sensations (i.e. feelings of hunger or pain); and the third, *badīhiyyāt*, self-evident propositions or principles (i.e. the whole is greater than its part). The most common form of the latter is the knowledge that *al-nafī wa-l-ithbāt lā yajtami'ān wa-lā yartafi'ān*, affirmation and negation cannot coexist. For Rāzī, the most self-evident of all self-evident propositions (*ajlā al-badīhiyyāt*) is the knowledge that a thing either exists or does not exist, *al-shay' immā an yakūna wa-immā an lā yakūn*.[137] In a series of ambiguous devil's advocate assertions purported to embody the sceptical approach of those that would deny the *badīhiyyāt* as being uncertain, and the *ḥissiyyāt* as the only viable avenue of certain knowledge, Rāzī puts forward arguments on behalf of this hypothetical party. These do not constitute an attack *per se* on the *badīhiyyāt*, at least directly, but moreover are an attempt to undermine the notions of practical certainty,[138] and by extension the certitude engendered by self-evident propositions. Ṭūsī in his *Talkhīṣ*, one should remember, dispels these contentions showing them to be sophistries.

In one of these contentions, Rāzī restates the most self-evident proposition in the form *al-nafī wa-l-ithbāt lā yajtami'ān wa-lā yartafi'ān*,[139] everything either exists or does not exist and nothing can be both existent and non-existent. The principle for Rāzī revolves around existence and non-existence. This perhaps may be explained by recognizing that the first act of knowledge is of reality in its actuality, *wujūd* as a universal. Once this is grasped, the concomitance, so to speak, of this apprehension is to grasp or become aware of the distinction between what is intuitively apprehended, namely, *wujūd* (existence), and its contradiction, *'adam* (non-existence). This is because it is only on apprising oneself of this distinction that one is then able to say that something particular *is* rather than *is not*.

Another way of understanding this is to analyse the notion of the relation of being, which underlies all other ideas. When one attempts to think of something, one thinks of that thing as possessing being, or else it cannot be thought of. The notion of being therefore is the primary object of thought and is at the basis of all thought. Following from this, any primary principle must equally exhibit a primary relation with being. If we say relation, then the relation of being must be to something else that is distinct from being, as any relation is a relation between two distinct entities. That which is distinct from being, other than being, must of necessity be not-being. The primary principle must, then, following the former analysis, express a relation between *wujūd* and *'adam*. This relation is a relation of contradiction between one thing and another, and hence we arrive at the PNC. This principle also provides us with the first division of being, as every division is made through its opposites, and every opposition proceeds through affirmation and negation.

One of the contentions put forward by Rāzī regarding what he names as *awwal al-awā'il*, the first of the first, the PNC as stipulated above, is that there must be a *taṣawwur* of both parts (*al-ṭarafayn*) of the proposition for it to be assented to. This is because *taṣdīq* relates to judgements, which in turn presuppose *taṣawwur*. There is only *taṣawwur*, however, if a thing can be known. If it cannot be known, there cannot be *taṣawwur*, and consequently no judgement following Rāzī's *ghayr al-ma'lūm yamtani' al-ḥukm 'alayhi*, no judgement can be made on that which is not known.[140] One part of the proposition concerns non-existence. Non-existence does not exist, and what does not exist cannot be known or predicated of, and if it cannot be known, there cannot be any *taṣawwur* of it. According to the sceptical contention advanced by Rāzī, everything conceivable is distinct (*mutamayyiz*), and if *mutamayyiz*, then *muta'ayyin* (individuated) by itself, and every individuated thing by itself is affirmed in itself, *kull muta'ayyin fī nafsihi fa-huwa thābit fī nafsihi*.[141] Ījī adds that all that is distinct is certain.[142] If the non-existent is conceivable, the non-existent would then be certain, which is absurd. If the non-existent is inconceivable, as per Rāzī, on the basis that all that can be conceived is distinct and affirmable in itself (*fa-kull mutaṣawwarin thābit fī nafsihi*), and that which has no *thubūt* cannot be conceived, and the non-existent has no *thubūt* and consequently cannot be conceived; then this nevertheless, according to Ījī, entails the conception of the non-existent. To declare the non-existent inconceivable is to conceive of it, which again is absurd. This approximates part of the solution that Ṭūsī offers to this seeming paradox.[143]

Ṭūsī first states that *al-nafī huwa raf' al-ithbāt*, negation is to remove affirmation, and then critically, *wa-raf' al-ithbāt lā yakūn 'ayn al-ithbāt*, removing affirmation is not itself an affirmation, and the negation of extramental existence is an affirmation in mental existence related to the extramental non-existence, *ithbāt dhihnī mansūb ilā lā ithbāt khārijī*. In the mind this conception is distinct and individuated in itself and affirmed or exists in the mind. If this is so, then to state that the non-existent is absolutely inconceivable is false, because it is conceived from the perspective that it is extramentally non-existent.[144] In essence, a concept of something, and that which it is a conception of, are two separate entities. In reply to Rāzī's presentation of the denial of the possibility of predication for that which is unknown, Ṭūsī adopts the view that the predication of the impossibility of predication *is* itself an act of predication.[145] This is one way of reading the paradox. It should be said, though, that this is not the only way to construe the paradox.[146]

The PNC consists of stating that there is a pair of judgements, such that both cannot be true (the principle of identity); neither can both judgements be false (the principle of the excluded middle). If one objects to the principle in this form, then either the proposer or the objector is right, in which case the principle is vindicated. All knowledge makes a claim on truth, and thus every judgement involves an agent that is the subject engaged in the act of making that judgement. If this statement were to be denied by someone, then such a claim would be unjustified because it would be positing *itself* as a claim to truth. If it were to be posited, then, that truth does not exist, then this line of thinking negates itself by way of contradiction. That is to say, if the existence of truth is denied, then the truth does not exist. If the truth does not exist, then it is true that the truth does not exist, therefore truth does exist. In reply to Kant, one may legitimately, then, wonder whether it is merely necessary to be convinced of the mind's capability, rather than to hold it sufficient for the mind to be actually capable of discovering truth with certitude as an implicit natural and spontaneous conviction.

Ibn Sīnā expounds various versions of the PNC, which he refers to as one of the *aqāwīl al-ṣādiqa* to which everything that exists returns, notably in its form of the principle of the excluded middle in the *Ilāhiyyāt*,[147] *lā wāsiṭa bayn al-ījāb wa-l-salb*; there is no intermediary between affirmation and negation, the two contradictories cannot be simultaneously absent from a given subject. Another construction of the PNC he utilizes is rather more well known: *al-ījāb wa-l-salb lā yajtamiʿān wa-lā yaṣduqān maʿan ... wa-lā yartafiʿān wa-lā yakdhibān maʿan*[148] (affirmation and negation do not combine and are not both true together ... and that both cannot simultaneously be removed and denied). A cannot both be A and not A whilst being A, but also *the same attribute cannot be in the same instance affirmed and denied of the same subject.* The time element, once again, refers to a simultaneous formal relation and not to a particularized instance of time as the principle is beyond time. Furthermore, contraries are not contradictions, but are constituted of things that are albeit different and disparate from each other but pertain to the same genus. Contrary opposition is marked by a differentiation in quality only, contraries being incompatible only as regards their truth and not their falsehood, unlike contradictories. They are not mutually inferable like contradictories.

We can thus state that contradiction is one of the oppositions, namely, one of the four relations, which comprise contradiction (*tanāquḍ*), contrariety (*taḍādd*),[149] subcontrariety (*dākhilatān taḥt al-taḍādd*), and subalternation (*tadākhul*),[150] that Ibn Sīnā distinguishes on the basis of difference of truth-values (see figure 1).

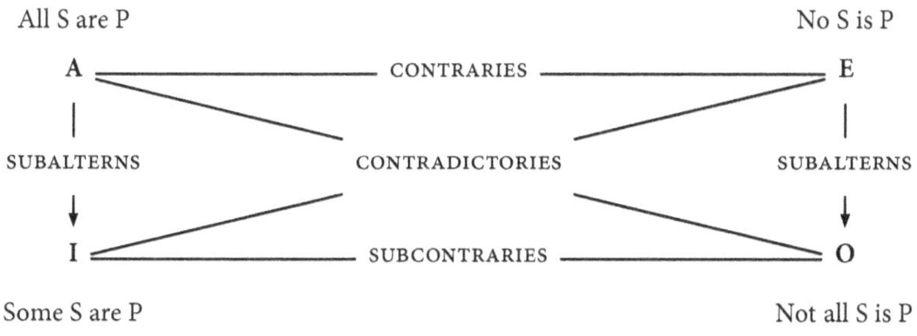

Figure 1

In accordance with this, Ibn Sīnā presents contradiction as corresponding to classical negation, contrariety to incompatibility, subcontrariety to inclusive disjunction (*qaḍiyya sharṭiyya munfaṣila*),[151] and subalternation to implication, 'P implies Q'. There are four relations expressed by the square of opposition. Contradiction (*tanāquḍ*): the relation between a universal and the particular of a different quality, A and O, E and I. So, to be more exacting and using the square above, A, a universal affirmative proposition and the corresponding particular negative, I, both having the same subject and predicate, are contradictories. Alternatively, one can oppose in contradiction a particular affirmative, I, and a universal negative, E. Contrariety (*taḍādd*): the relation between a universal and the universal of a different quality, A and E. Subalternation (*tadākhul*): the relation between a universal and the particular of the same quality, A and I, E and O. Subcontrariety (*dākhilatān taḥt al-taḍādd*): the relation between a particular and a particular of a different quality, I and O.

In the *Tahdhīb*, it states that for there to be a contradiction there must be a difference in quantity (*kamm*), quality (*kayf*), and modality or perspective (*jiha*); comprising the necessary (*wājib*), impossible (*mumtaniʿ*), and possible (*mumkin*).[152] This is where the two propositions have to differ in these aforementioned three. The propositions in mind would be more precisely *ḥamliyya maḥṣūra*, restrictive attributive propositions. It is important to take heed of the structure of the opposition of contradiction and the difference between it and a contrary, one that Hegel failed to heed in his logic. For there to be a contradiction, there must be agreement of the two propositions on everything except affirmation (*ījāb*), negation (*salb*), and quantifier (*sūr*). The latter are four in number as stated in the *ʿIbāra*, namely, all (*kull*), none (*lā shayʾ*), some (*baḍ*), not all (*lā kull*).[153] The matters necessitating propositional agreement are known as the *al-waḥdāt al-thamāniyya* (the eight unities): subject, *mawdūʿ*; the predicate, *maḥmūl*; the apposition, *iḍāfa*; condition, *sharṭ*; the whole and the part, *al-kull wa-l-juzʾ*; actuality and potentiality, *al-fiʿl wa-l-quwwa*; time, *zamān*; space, *makān*.[154] These are later reduced by the post-classical tradition to two unities that are held to include all the others, namely, subject and predicate.

Since contradiction (*tanāquḍ*) is the relation between affirmation and denial, the denial of the truth of a proposition is the same as the assertion of the truth of its contradictory. Also, to assert the truth of a proposition is to deny the truth of its contradictory. In order to contradict a proposition, therefore, one only needs to assert the minimum necessary to collapse the truth of that proposition. We can further state that two contradictories have to deny and affirm the same thing about the same thing under the same respect. This provides us with the result that one contradictory must be false under the PNC, and one of the contradictories must be true under the principle of the excluded middle. When one part of the contradiction is adverted to in the traditional texts, what is being expressed is one of two contradictory judgements. These two parts, or two contradictory judgements, exhaust the possibilities as there is no middle ground, no median position between them. Contraries do not, in contrast, exhaust the possibilities by their opposition.

Contrary opposition (*takhāluf*), as was stated above, is marked by a difference of quality alone. Contraries cannot be true together, and *may* be false together. If we look at the square of opposition above, we can ascertain that if A is true, then I is true due to subalternation. Following this, if I is true, then E must be false by way of contradiction. We can now see that if A is true, then E is false. Conversely, if E is true, then A is false. Contraries, therefore, cannot be true together. Contraries may be false together or not, because no inference can be made about each of the pair. Contrary propositions are thus only incompatible with, but not alternative to, each other.

Subcontrary opposition is an opposition between two propositions, I and O, which are of opposite quality. They cannot be false together, and they may be true together; alternately, one may be true and both may be true together. If they were false together, then contradictories would be false together, which is impossible. This is because if they were false together, then A and E, by way of subalternation, would both be false, which means two respective contradictories of I and O being false together. Subcontraries may be true together, but the truth of a subcontrary does not allow any inference as to the truth or falsehood of the other. This can be verified in the following way: if I is *assumed* to be true, its status being doubtful, then E is false (as the contradictory), and A (as the subalternate) may be true or false. Thus, the status of I, as true or false, still may not be inferred. This also shows that the PNC does not apply to subcontraries, since they may be true together, being imperfect oppositions. I and O are, respectively, subalterns of A and E, as the truth of the particular proposition is derived from the truth of the universal proposition.[155]

The main argument we wish to restate and reiterate once again is that the PNC is not primarily a principle or law of propositions, nor of judgements, but a principle of being. As stated earlier, there is an indelible link between logical necessity and ontological necessity, and it is this which we wish to explore.

It is rather a principle of propositions only by derivation. This can be easily ascertained, as when we examine the prohibition against contradictory propositions, we find that it applies only when propositions are being used to express contradictory judgements. We can further state that the PNC is primarily a principle of judgements only by derivation, since if it were primarily a principle of judgements, then judgements could never be contradictory, which they naturally and obviously can be. Judgements are capable of being contradicted. It is also a principle of judgements by derivation because all judgements intend being, and if so, such an intention means that all judgements affirm being to that which is, and deny being to that which is not. On this basis, since all judgements intend being, are subject to being, and being cannot be contradictory, then contradictory judgements cannot be simultaneously true.[156]

The PNC is thus primarily and fundamentally a principle of being. It is a principle of judgements by derivation from the principle of being, and it is a principle of propositions by derivation from the principle of judgements. This can be illustrated by stating that propositions should not be contradictory since such contradictory propositions are the external expression of contradictory judgements; and judgements must not be contradictory because all judgements intend being; and being cannot be contradictory. That which is, is, and that which is not, is not.

To reiterate once more, the PNC applies to propositions only when they are used to express judgements. The PNC applies to judgements because judgements intend being, in the sense that they affirm that being is being. The PNC applies to being by an intrinsic necessity because, as stated above, being cannot be non-being (the principle of identity). Logical necessity is therefore an intellectual accession to ontological necessity. One can even go further and state that all logical necessity is in a prior sense ontological. Logical positivists introduced the idea that the necessity of logic arose from linguistic convention. This in turn led to the acceptance of the PNC as a law of language, but as stated earlier, however, the PNC is a principle of propositions by derivation from the principle of judgements and thus with necessary entailments. What this implies is that if propositions are not expressing judgements, then they may be verbally self-contradictory or contradictory. If they express judgements, they cannot be contradictory, subject to the rules set out above governing contradictions. The function of language is primarily to express meaning, which is completed by the act of judgement, and thus language is necessarily subject to the laws of judgement. Since judgements, however, intend being, language is subject to the laws of being and thus the PNC. The PNC imposes itself on judgement by its existential priority, which in turn imposes itself on propositions, moulded by the rules of language, which provides us with the logical necessity of analytical propositions. This is the line of priority that displays once again the connection between logical necessity and ontological necessity.

It was stated earlier that *wujūd* represented the first intuition one could have, a self-evident reality that forces itself on one as a conception (*taṣawwur*). It is this fundamental intuition of being that becomes expressed in propositional form as the principle of identity[157] (*kull shay' huwa nafsuhu*) and the PNC. This intuition is also the first step in man's cognitive system, *wujūd* being intelligible, otherwise there could not be a *taṣawwur* of it. If *wujūd* is intelligible, that is to say, *wujūd* is the object of our intellect, then it means that every thing in existence has a reason, has intelligibility, an intelligibility that we may aspire to. It is also critical following our argument that we understand that what is being posited here is that *wujūd* or being imposes itself on the cognitive process, and that its necessities become the necessities of this process also. The act of understanding thus is prescribed by those existential necessities. It is being that imposes necessity into the cognitive process by dictating the principles for the pursuit of truth. It is this intelligibility, we contend, that can serve as a basis for a realist metaphysics.

The discussion of self-evident principles here encompasses a rational understanding and examination, indemonstrable as a whole in itself, but nevertheless certain and capable of evincing conviction and certitude by way of rational principles. Whether ultimately that is enough to manifest an operative certitude, operative in the theological sense, rather than, say, a pyrrhic certitude or a barren conclusion, is another matter.

The Teleological Dimension

Objections to the Principle of Non-contradiction

One of the consequences of illustrating the ontological nature of the PNC is the commitment that the principle represents as a law of being and not merely a logical instrument. If this is the case, what is to be made of the denigrators of the principle at the logical level, whether it is advanced on a subrational, rational, or supra-rational basis? In the first category, the school of dialetheism and the methodology of paraconsistent logic will be examined in relation to specifically Nicolai Vasiliev's imaginary logic and his main objection to the PNC. For the second and third categories, the meeting of Ibn 'Arabī with Ibn Rushd will be examined as it has long been held out to advance the invalidity of the PNC at a particular juncture of elevated spiritual discourse. It is hoped that the examination of the two examples will bear out our contentions in the previous section.

Dialetheism and Paraconsistent Logic

The paradox of dialetheistic literature is that, on the one hand, the PNC is decried and denied, and with the same breath is used implicitly or explicitly to do so. Putting that simple fact to the side, the basis of this section is to draw out the rationale, if any, for this particular philosophical standpoint in one instance. There is much debate as to whether multi-value logic or paraconsistent logic draws its heritage from Nikolai Aleksandrovich Vasiliev, but they both at least consider him a founding father. To that end, his seminal viewpoint on the PNC will be primarily examined before proceeding to look at paraconsistency in relation to its indebtedness to Kantianism. Dialetheism denies propositional bivalence and contravalence, that for any proposition, respectively, it is either true or false (principle of the excluded middle); it is not both true and false (PNC). The proponents of such logic put forward the liar paradox as an example for this rejection, and even claim anteriority for such rejection in Aristotle's famous treatment of future contingents, that is to say, the question of whether it is true or false that a future event, a sea-battle in this case, will take place. Aristotle's deliberation on this led him to state that the principle of bivalence does not apply until one of the two options, namely, there will be, or there will not be, a sea-battle, comes to pass. Until the determination of this, the principle in effect does not apply.[158]

A word should be said primarily about the liar paradox, whose earliest form perhaps is that illustrated by the proposition 'All Cretans are liars', spoken by a Cretan, Epimenedes, and known as Epimenedes' paradox. If the proposition is true, then Epimenedes, a Cretan, is a liar, therefore the proposition is false, because he is lying, therefore not all Cretans are liars. But having said that, he is a Cretan, and if the proposition is true, then all Cretans are liars, and therefore the proposition is true. This is the basis of the contradiction embedded in the liar paradox. This is referred to in the *kalām* tradition as the fallacy (*mughālaṭa*) of *al-jadhr al-aṣamm*, the irrational root. A recent publication in Iran by Ahad Qaramaleki has usefully collected together the treatment of this subject in one volume by figures such as Jalāl al-Dīn al-Dawānī and Ṣadr al-Dīn al-Dashtakī.[159] Taftāzānī has also dealt with this fallacy in his *Sharḥ al-Maqāṣid*, a treatment that set the scene for rebuttals and explorations by the respective authors mentioned before.[160]

The paradox is introduced by Taftāzānī in the context of his discussion on the divine command theory of ethics, specifically regarding the question of whether lying is always wrong or not. The context of this debate revolved around the Muʿtazilī assertion by Qāḍī ʿAbd al-Jabbār that lying was always to be considered ethically wrong. The upshot of his discussion is to say that no solution may be proffered for this paradox.[161] In disagreement with Taftāzānī as to its insolubility, and in reference to Epimenedes, one can arrive at a satisfactory result by applying the rules governing contradictions. In the first place, the statement 'All Cretans are liars' as asserted is not contradictory. The fact that Epimenedes, a Cretan, says this means that he is either speaking truthfully or falsely. If he is speaking the truth, then he will be speaking falsely following the assertion. If he is speaking falsely, then he is being true to the assertion that all Cretans speak falsely. The problem here is that the premises of the argument are implicitly contradictory: on the one hand, Cretans always lying, and on the other, a Cretan making the assertion. The result of this is that we arrive at an explicit contradiction. One of the two premises therefore can only be true, but not both together. The PNC is thus not challenged.[162]

Turning to paraconsistency, in 1910, the Russian philosopher Nicolai Vasiliev published *On Partial Judgements,* wherein he set out the idea of what he termed 'an imaginary logic' that would be non-Aristotelian, rejecting the fundamental principles of the PNC, the principle of the excluded middle, and by implication the principle of identity. In 1912, he published his seminal article 'Imaginary (Non-Aristotelian) Logic',[163] wherein he attempted to present the idea of a non-Aristotelian logic, in other words, pleading for logical pluralism. Interestingly and somewhat ironically, he states in the article:

> The subject matter of imaginary (non-Aristotelian) logic is a logical world and logical operations different from ours. Formulae of both logics are mutually contradictory: the truth of the formulae of imaginary logic excludes the truth of formulae of our Aristotelian logic, and vice versa. Consequently, they both cannot be true in one and the same world; if Aristotelian logic is true in our world, then non-Aristotelian logic can be true only in a different world. This contradictory, mutually exclusive relation between the two logics, their difference not only in content but also in subject matter, is a reason to call

this 'new logic' non-Aristotelian logic. In calling it 'imaginary', we would (also) want to point to another peculiarity. Our logic is the logic of reality, in the sense that it is a tool for knowledge of this reality, and thus is closely connected with it. The new logic does not have such a connection with our reality; it is a purely ideal construction. Only in a world different from ours, in an imaginary world (the basic properties of which we can, nevertheless, exactly define) imaginary logic could be a tool for knowledge.[164]

The irony is precisely in the attempt to define or describe an alternate system of logic in reliance on 'Aristotelian' operations of logic. To put it bluntly, he invokes, ad hominem, the PNC to distinguish the two systems. His purporting to describe the imaginary world utilizes the logical operations of 'Aristotelian' logic, which seems to contradict entirely the basis of his suppositions. As Lobachevski is deemed to have devised non-Euclidean geometry, Euclidean geometry without the fifth postulate of the axiom of parallel lines, which at one point he called imaginary geometry, Vasiliev purports to advance a non-Aristotelian logic without the PNC.[165] To do this, Vasiliev first defines the PNC as that which asserts the *incompatibility* between an assertion and its negation, on the basis that where there is no incompatibility, there can be no negation. Since negation is that which is incompatible with affirmation, the PNC is implicated in the definition of negation and, according to Vasiliev, the PNC can never consequently be violated by our thought processes.[166]

Vasiliev, though, has a particular understanding of the PNC, and a particular differentiation between negation and incompatibility. Although he concedes that negation can never coincide with affirmation, his conception of negation, reducible to incompatibility, is based on an incompatibility of predicates.

> Since the law of contradiction is a consequence of the definition of negation, constructing a logic without the law of contradiction amounts to constructing a logic without our negation which is reducible to incompatibility.[167]

He explains that a negative proposition, for example, 'S is not P', has two aspects, a formal and a material one. The formal is that the negative proposition states the falsehood of the affirmative proposition 'S is P'. The material is that the negative proposition is based on the incompatibility of predicates. He continues:

> One should accurately distinguish between these two aspects. The formal aspect manifests [the fact] that the truth of a negative proposition implies the recognition of the falsehood of the affirmative one, but it leaves open the question on what grounds we can ascertain the truth of negative propositions. The material aspect gives an answer to this question. Therefore, the formal aspect manifests the properties of negation; the material aspect manifests the grounds for negation. While preserving the formal aspect, we can change the material one and then obtain a different kind of negation.
>
> Only our affirmative propositions about objects and facts are immediate, that is, based on perception and sensation; the negative ones are always inferred.[168]

Affirmative propositions about objects and facts, based on the senses and perception, are deemed immediate, with negative propositions always inferred. This is so since the affirmation can be seized immediately by the senses. The negative proposition has to be inferred on the basis of incompatibility or on the basis of other inference. Vasiliev states that the imaginary logic he envisages would allow for negative propositions to be also immediate as much as affirmative ones, 'where experience itself would convince us without any inference that "S is not P"'.[169] What Vasiliev is trying to arrive at in imaginary logic is the severance of the link between negation and incompatibility, in order to allow the coincidence of an affirmative proposition and a negative proposition at the same time. This is a world where the PNC does not exist, in a sense only, as we shall see, as negation operates without its implicit or explicit use. An affirmative proposition may therefore be declared false by a negative proposition without a resort to incompatibility.[170]

As can be easily noticed, Vasiliev eschews the use of the PNC, by stating that the nature of negation espoused excludes it, as its negation is not based on incompatibility. The latter is the basis of the negation envisaged by the PNC. This is an error, though, as incompatibility is appropriate in the context of contraries where opposition is not absolute as in contradiction. A contradictory, taking the principle into consideration, is not incompatible; it is utterly inadmissible. Vasiliev, perhaps, then, disingenuously or in a pique of the imagination, declares that the PNC and what he terms the law of the absolute difference between truth and falsehood must be distinguished. The former may, according to him, be rejected, but the latter may not be avoided or dismissed.[171] In referring to the law of absolute difference, he states:[172]

> The law of absolute difference between truth and falsehood applies to the cognizing subject and forbids him/her to contradict him/herself; [it] indicates that a true proposition is always true, and a false one always false, and that therefore he/she cannot declare one and the same proposition now true, now false. This law forbids self-contradiction; [it] imposes 'self-consistency', the coherence of propositions of the cognizing subject. Therefore, it could be called the law of 'non-self-contradiction'.

For Vasiliev, the law of absolute difference is at the basis of his imaginary logic, providing the law with a subjective value alone. To clarify, his notion of the PNC applies to the world of objects, but he declares that contradictory predicates may not be realized there because no grounds can simultaneously exist to furnish affirmative and negative propositions about them, and thus no contradictions arise in the real world.[173] Very simply this means that if Zayd is stated to be a human being and not a human being simultaneously, then Vasiliev would accept that the PNC has been violated, but if he affirms this and holds to it consistently, then he does not violate the law of absolute difference between truth and falsehood. This is what can be termed the law of non-self-contradiction. Vasiliev further states that propositions should be divided into three types, affirmative 'S is A', negative 'S is not A', and indifferent 'S is A and S is not A'.

Before we examine the basis of this third proposition in Kant's understanding of opposition, we should recognize that by the PNC, Vasiliev means Kant's formulation of it, namely: 'No predicate contradictory of a thing can belong to it.'[174] This was formulated by Kant in this way, also namely as a principle of predication, to avoid the reference to time, as discussed above. The Kantian form adopted by Vasiliev is the logical expression of the principle referring to a mental act by which we judge the respective thing. Negation here is thus reduced to a predicamental level alone. It is this formulation of the principle, which he holds to be the proper form of the principle, that is declared to be invalid in the intelligible world, as it derives its force from the experience of the existence of incompatible predicates, and therefore remaining unassailable solely in the world of experience.

There is much conflation here once again, as the matter relates back to the Kantian understanding of opposites, which was treated by him in his pre-critical phase in a 1763 article concerning negative quantities in philosophy.[175] What is of interest in this latter article is the distinction which Kant sets out between logical and real contradiction. As was said above, Vasiliev's third proposition is indebted to Kant's formulation of opposition, which is of two types, logical and real. His categorization of the former is that it is the simultaneous predication of a predicate 'P' and its negative 'not P' of 'S'. This simultaneity negates the possibility of 'S', the denial of the subject being a contradiction. Real opposition is different, though.

Real opposition, according to Kant, exists where two predicates of a thing are opposed, but not as contradictories. Both predicates, though in reality opposed to each other, are affirmative, but in opposite senses, like an active obligation and an equal passive obligation; its result is the *nihil privativum, repraesentabile,* which Kant terms nothing or zero, as they cancel themselves out; however, the nothing is not the logical nothing but rather an equilibrium. The two predicates simultaneously apply to the subject. The difference here between logical opposition and real opposition is that both predicates are affirmative in the latter. To clarify, this second form of opposition concerns two predicates in a subject that are opposed but not by way of the PNC, since the cancellation of one predicate by the other leads to something rather than the pure nothing of logical contradiction. Kant also uses the example of the simultaneity of a motive force (that which impels something to move) of a body in one direction and an equal tendency of that body in an opposite direction as not being in contradiction as predicates. He states that they are both possible in one body occurring simultaneously, and that the result is not contradiction, but that the two forces bring the body to rest. In the case of logic, Kant states that the quality of 'in motion' and 'not in motion' would be contradictory and lead to an absurdity. In real opposition, the opposite concept does not destroy or annihilate its opposite, but rather leads to a physical state called 'rest' or 'equilibrium'.[176]

> It is rather the case that both predicates, A and B, are affirmative. However, since the consequences of the two, each construed as existing on its own, would be a and b, it follows that, if the two are construed as existing together, neither consequence a nor consequence b is to be found in the subject; the consequence of the two predicates A and B, construed as existing together, is therefore zero … On the other hand, in the case of cancellation through contradiction it is absolutely nothing which exists.[177]

What Kant is asserting is that in phenomenal reality the agreement between one thing and another is not based on non-contradiction, but on a model of equilibrium, where two opposing forces can come together in a subject without one of them dominating the other. So that in 'real' opposition the subject subsists, but the predicate effects cancel each other out. In contradiction, however, there is no subject affirmed. This, we contend, is the origin of the chasm that is subsequently opened between logical truth and ontological truth, a separation enshrined by the distinction between the formal and transcendental logic in the *Critique of Pure Reason,* and moreover, the basis of Vasiliev's understanding of negation.

The predicates here are inherences in the same subject which are mutually exclusive, but they do not deny the subject in any case if one is negated. It is true that opposition is a second intention, since things in extramental existence are not contradictory; they are just there, existing. In that sense, talk of contradiction is a propositional matter as Kant contends. This is in line, however, with the refusal to understand the ontological form of the PNC, hence the attested unworkability of applying a logical form of the principle to reality. The other glaring issue one may notice is that the Kantian form of real opposition, expressed albeit in terms of propositions, becomes subject to the laws of thought and thus must be analysed in accordance with them. If this is the case, then what we have before us is a mechanistic reductionism that cannot be transposed onto social forces or political movements, for example, as the term force is used with a clear Newtonian bias. His example of real opposition is also the same as saying that there is a ground in a concrete continuum where it is not true that it is A and not A, or alternatively that it is both A and not A. We are surely, then, speaking of contraries and not contradictions by any stretch of the imagination.

The reformulation of the PNC by Kant, and upon which the whole of Vasiliev's reasoning may be said to be posited, is essentially stating that a contradiction may only occur between 'S' and 'P' of an A, E, I, O categorical proposition. The reason he reformulates, or reduces, the PNC down to a principle of predication based on the logical form of a categorical proposition is because of his opposition to the time element in the classical formulation, which he sees as extraneous to logic as it limits the assertions of the PNC by time relations.[178] This again is problematic, since to hold that time is extraneous to logic is, strictly speaking, wrong. Time is a purely logical concept, in abstract, which by relation is necessarily rooted in ontological reality. We say 'by relation' because it is contiguous with the existence of contingent beings, without which there would be no time, so to speak, but simply an everlasting now. Time is essentially, then, an expression of the successive changes that occur in contingent beings and nothing more.

The objection, then, in the *Critique of Pure Reason* is to the formulation 'it is impossible that something should at one and the same time both be and not be.' If the principle is taken to mean that judgements opposed by way of contradiction cannot be true at the same time, then Kant has a point. This is because it is uncertain whether the relation of time refers to the judgements themselves as acts of thought or merely to their content.[179] If it refers to acts of thought, then the formulation is obviously deficient and does not deliver the requirement for strict opposition that contradiction demands. This is because the same thing may be thought of differently across a time span, but nevertheless remain the same thing. If it is the second, then it means that judgements that are contradictory cannot both be true insofar as their content refers to one and the same time. If the content agrees in some things, but not as it happens in the determination of time, then the formulation is once again deficient, as it does not provide the strict form of opposition required for contradiction.

Kant's reformulation also leads to the conclusions he adopts regarding the domain or extent of the principle. Primarily it is characterized as, and reduced to, a principle of judgement, a reduction that was demonstrably rejected above, and second, is limited in its application to the domain of logic alone.

> The proposition that no predicate contradictory of a thing can belong to it, is entitled the principle of contradiction, and is a universal, though merely negative, criterion of all truth. For this reason it belongs only to logic. It holds of knowledge, merely as knowledge in general, irrespective of content; and asserts that the contradiction completely cancels and invalidates it …
>
> The principle of contradiction must therefore be recognised as being the universal and completely sufficient principle of all analytic knowledge; but beyond the sphere of analytic knowledge it has, as a sufficient criterion of truth, no authority and no field of application.[180]

The reduction of the PNC to its logical formulation as a categorical proposition, as above, leads to the result that one may have two predicates in a subject that negate each other without violating the form of the Kantian PNC, so long as the two predicates do not negate the subject (namely, the thing). The second element to note is also found in the same section of the *Critique of Pure Reason*.[181]

> But … [the principle] … allows of a positive employment, not merely, that is, to dispel falsehood and error, but also for the knowing of truth. For, if the judgment is analytic, whether negative or affirmative, its truth can always be adequately known in accordance with the principle of contradiction. The reverse of that which as concept is contained and is thought in the knowledge of the object, is always rightly denied. But since the opposite of the concept would contradict the object, the concept itself must necessarily be affirmed of it.

Kant here establishes that the condition for a categorical proposition to be considered analytic, is that 'its truth can always be adequately known in accordance with the principle of contradiction.' This means that that which contradicts the subject in an analytic categorical proposition is denied, and that that which is contained in the subject is affirmed. If this cannot be done, then the proposition is not analytic. Kant gives an example where this may not be done, 'If I say that a man who is unlearned is not learned …', then neither predicate denies the subject, and one must add 'at one and the same time', for there to be a contradiction between the predicates.[182] He then adds that if he were to say, 'No unlearned man is learned,' the proposition becomes analytic, since the property of *unlearnedness* goes to make up the subject, so that learned contradicts the subject and not merely a predicate. In other words, the negative judgement becomes clear as a consequence of the PNC without any need to use 'at one and the same time'.[183]

To recapitulate, therefore, the PNC following Kant loses its validity in the intelligible world since it derives its power from the world of experience, namely, the experience of the established existence of incompatible predicates. It is also, in effect, unquestionable only in the world of experience. In the context of Vasiliev, who inherits these contentions, the law of absolute difference between truth and falsehood, or what is termed the law of non-self-contradiction, in contrast to the PNC, preserves its validity also in relation to the intelligible world. The question that arises, though, is that when the law of absolute difference recites the categories of truth and falsehood in its formula, by which criteria are we to measure the truth and falsehood in extramental reality? The traditional understanding of the PNC is that it possesses a logical form, a psychological form, and an ontological form. The logical we have dealt with, the psychological is that it is necessary of anything either to affirm or deny. The ontological form is essentially the principle of identity, 'each being is exclusively itself.' This is completely in line with cosmological realism, which asserts that each being is unique, not interchangeable, not expendable.

It is true that the intellect, when knowing a thing, cannot be separated from that thing in the act of knowing. For Kant, this implies a projection of the intellect onto that thing, an idealist prioritization of the mind rather than the ontological nature of the object of knowledge, namely, being. This in essence is the position of conceptualism and which leads directly to scepticism since it makes all true knowledge impossible. In this schema, all ideas are formed by the mind within its own structure, without there being any input from reality in the formation of the idea. In the traditional understanding, following upon the doctrine of real definitions, ideas are not simply thoughts but *taṣawwurāt,* which are apprehensions of essences.[184] Thoughts are the process or the pronouncement stemming from ideas, culminating in judgements. Furthermore, the proposition is the expression of the judgement, where the validity of the judgement is in direct proportion to the objectivity of the ideas. It is true that the judgement is an expression of the relation between ideas, but its validity is dependent on those ideas being objective. Vasiliev's so-called absolute law of non-self-contradiction unfortunately, though, remains subsumed to the cardinal Kantian principle of conceptualism.

In the corrective traditional understanding, by contrast, the intellect, in making the judgement, implies its power to know the reality it represents in the judgement. This capacity or power of the intellect to apprehend being gives rise to the notion that every being that exists is intelligible. This expresses the reality that being is capable of moving the passive intellect to represent it intentionally in the mind. This capacity to move the intellect is commensurate with the being's degree of intelligibility. What we are saying essentially is that intelligibility parallels existence, the degree of existence determining the degree of intelligibility, and necessarily so, since *no thing* principially can be unintelligible. The truth of a thing thus is its degree of existence, its being. The difference between this and logical truth is equally clear, as logical truth is the intellect's prior agreement or conformity with the thing it is capable of representing intentionally within itself. This does not, however, exhaust its intelligibility within an ontological framework.

We stated earlier that intelligibility parallels existence, and necessarily so. The necessity arises from the earlier-stated principle of identity, as a rejection of this intelligibility involves a rejection of the principle, since the predicate, intelligible, is one that adheres to the essence of being as subject. To reject this essential predicate is to reject or deny the subject, namely, being. It is therefore an essential predicate that is precisely exclusive to being. If it were not, it would then also be predicable of non-being. This would mean that the property of intelligible would apply both to being and non-being, that is to say, that the intellect would hold that the essential property attaches equally to being and non-being, so that being becomes also non-being, because intelligibility parallels existence. But 'being is not non-being' as the PNC tells us, and 'being is being' as the principle of identity tells us, so 'intelligible' may not be predicated of non-being and belongs exclusively to being.

'Yes and No'

In the consideration of various contemporary writers on the relationship of spiritual disclosure of knowledge (*kashf*), and reason (*'aql*), many antipathies have been raised that seem to suggest that the laws of logic do not pertain to the fruits of *mukāshafāt*. If, as we have contended and attempted to demonstrate above, the principles of logic were complementary of ontological principles, the stance of these latter writers would suggest confusion between the truth of the principles of logic and their use. If we look at the PNC, one can find no better illustration of this confusion than in the interpretation often heard or read of the meeting between Ibn 'Arabī, the saint and metaphysician, and the philosopher and *qāḍī* Ibn Rushd. The construction placed on this meeting revolves around the perceived separateness of logical reasoning and spiritual cognition. It is, in a sense, the view that the PNC ceases to be valid at a particular juncture of spiritually attained knowledge. It is important to underline and emphasize that there is a critical difference between the assertion that the PNC ceases to be valid, and that it ceases to apply. Where there is a resolution of contradictory opposites, where such opposites become undifferentiated, the PNC may cease to apply, but is never invalidated. At a particular resolution of reality, if one may speak this way, there are no contradictions, and consequently the principle in question does not apply. One often comes across Sufi literature wherein the author describes a state where opposites are resolved, or better still dissolved, due to *ḥayra* (bewilderment), and where often following upon hyperbolic intentions, the PNC is declared to be invalid. What is often meant here, though, is the presence of opposites whose degree of opposition is no longer apparent, in other words, opposites that are contraries occupying the same continuum, not contradictions, since contradictions do not inhabit degrees as they are perfect opposites.[185] What is also at issue is the point that indeterminacy cannot ground a contradictory opposition, whether it be an ontological or logical contradiction, since distinction is a necessary element of contradiction. The unity of opposites here is nothing more than the *coincidentia oppositorum*, the fundamental unity or resolution of opposites. This goes hand in hand with understanding that Ultimate Reality cannot be known, since being can never be exhausted by knowledge, which remains posterior and dependent on it. Only God can know Himself in His Ultimate Reality.

In the cosmology that Ibn ʿArabī adheres to, the realm of manifestation is the realm of opposites, duality, as separation is at the heart of manifestation. Everything that is manifested is dual and contingent as only God is One and Self-sufficient. The pairing of opposites that is found everywhere in creation illustrates this lack of sufficiency and hence duality. It is this duality that allows for distinction and differentiation, which Unity would dissolve, and thus allows for knowledge through polarities. To say manifestation is to say duality. This is essentially stating that things may be known through their contraries. Heat cannot be known without cold, light without darkness, life and death, subject and object. It is this polarity that the *ʿārifīn* transcend through *mukāshafa* or *mushāhada,* hence the 'union' of opposites perceived.

It was stated earlier that cosmological realism went hand in hand with epistemological realism. The denotation of the universe in the traditional Akbarian understanding is a series of correspondences between the different levels of creation (*marātib al-khalq*). Since Reality is One, there can be no real contradiction between one realm of existence and another, but rather a continuity between them. The logical realm cannot contradict the ontological, neither can a higher knowledge disavow a lower form of knowledge, as each operates at a designated level or degree in a harmonious correspondence. This notion of correspondence unites the internal realm of the human being with the outer cosmos, since everything that is brought into existence, by virtue of the agency of its existence, is tied and connected to everything else that shares this. It is on this basis that each of the parts of creation in its interior organization is analogous to each of the other parts, and hence one can perceive an order that subsists throughout all the levels of creation. It is this order that settles the hierarchies in the created world, including that of the sciences and of knowledge and epistemology as a whole, because cosmological presuppositions condition our theories of knowledge, and it should be added, theories of art.

This view of cosmology is by no means the domain of the theosophers alone. It is referred to widely in the Islamic intellectual tradition as *ʿilm al-āfāq wa-l-anfus* (the science of the horizons and souls), having been named so by ʿAlī ibn Abī Ṭālib, the Prophet's ﷺ cousin and son-in-law, according to the fourteenth-century Ashʿarī *mutakallim* Shams al-Dīn al-Samarqandī. The name of the science is said to refer back to the Qurʾanic verse 'We will show them Our proofs on the horizons (*sanurīhim ayātinā fī al-āfāqi*), and within themselves (*wa-fī anfusihim*), until they realize that it is the truth [or, "He is the Real"]' (Q41:53).

According to Samarqandī in his own treatise on cosmology titled *'Ilm al-āfāq wa-l-anfus*, cosmology is the science which examines existents (*mawjūdāt*) in order to attain knowledge of God.[186] This is in contrast to *ḥikma*, metaphysics, whose subject is existence qua existence, and also *kalām*, theology, whose subject matter relates to the central doctrines of faith. So, the subject (*mawdūʻ*) of the science of cosmology is existents, in as far as they manifest or indicate the qualities of God, in effect existents as signifiers of God. For Samarqandī, everything that has been created is a *maẓhar* (locus of manifestation) for the *Ḥaqq*, where signs of God that lead back to Him are manifested. In that respect, all sciences have as their goal the knowledge of God, and it is the duty of every *ʻāqil*[187] and an obligation on every mature person (*bāligh*) to pursue this goal by the three paths that he outlines.

The first path is that of those who follow the truthful words of God (i.e. revelation), *qawl al-ṣādiq*. The second path is the knowledge of things or existents in their reality and the knowledge of their contingency and reliance upon God. The third path is the purification of the soul by way of spiritual exercises and detachment from worldly pleasures.[188] Samarqandī states that the first path is *ẓāhir*, clear or obvious, and completes the other two. The second has to do with effects (*āthār*) of God's creation and that His perfection is manifest and clear in everything created. The paramount cosmological principle being expounded is namely that there is nothing created that does not manifest the signs of God's perfection and majesty.[189] This is pursuant to the verse referred to above (Q41:53) and also:

> Verily, in the creation of the heavens and the earth, and in the succession of night and day, there are indeed messages for all who are endowed with insight or discerning faculties, Such as those that [possess the innermost secrets] and remember Allah, standing, sitting, and reclining, and consider the creation of the heavens and the earth, [and say]: 'Our Lord! Thou created not this in vain. Glory be to Thee! Preserve us from the punishment of the Fire.' (Q3:190–91)

One must therefore seek to know the reality of things, as per the often quoted and popular statement attributed to the Prophet ﷺ: 'Lord, let us see things as they really are' (*Allāhumma arinā al-ashyāʾ kamā hiya*). This is in order to permit the practitioner of the science to discern the ontological nexus between existents and God, and in order to acquire true demonstrative certitude. This is *ʿilm al-āfāq*, the science of the horizons. The third path, *ʿilm al-anfus* (the science of souls), is the science of the purification of the heart so that the knowledge of oneself and one's internal states lead back to God.[190] The correspondence between the natural order and the signs of God (*āyāt Allāh*) informs the way that one views existence, namely, as a revelation. What the Qurʾan thus reveals through words directly is recapitulated as signs in the natural order, signs that allow us to know God, as in 'I created jinn and mankind only to worship Me' (Q51:56). Ibn ʿAjība, quoting Baqlī al-Shirāzī in his Qurʾanic commentary, *al-Baḥr al-madīd*, states that the meaning of 'to worship' in the latter verse is synonymous with 'to know'.[191] This also helps to distinguish the act of knowledge *per se*, that of the philosopher *simpliciter*, and the necessity for the presence of the Sharīʿah for the perfection of the act of knowledge.

The created order is hence the *maẓhar* of the Divine Names and Attributes by way of analogies between them and the world and the soul of the believer (*muʾmin*). Moreover, the most qualitative analogy between the microcosm and the macrocosm is established by way of *al-asmāʾ al-ilāhiyya* (the Divine Names). Each Name can be analysed in terms of its scope or breadth (*saʿa*), or the degree to which it is reflected within the phenomena in the world. Although each Name refers to Allah, 'Allah' is the *ism al-jāmiʿ* (the All-comprehensive Name) that contains all the Names in an undifferentiated mode. Each Name denotes the Divine Essence, *al-dhāt al-ilāhiyya*, but in terms of a specific relation that the Essence takes on with created things. Similarly, the world, as we have earlier stated, is a *maẓhar* for all the Names, and equally so with the human being. Ibn ʿArabī correspondingly calls the human being in the first chapter of the *Fuṣūs al-ḥikam, al-kawn al-jāmiʿ* (the all-comprehensive engendered thing).[192]

The respective verse in *Fuṣṣilat* is a clear indication that the human being shares or partakes in the panoply of the divine signs or signifiers, partaking in the sense that every sign being a truth has a reality that can be verified or realized by us. In the hadith of Ṣāliḥ ibn Mismār,[193] the Prophet ﷺ asked the Companion Ḥārith ibn Mālik al-Anṣārī: 'How are you?' (*kayfa anta*), or 'what are you [upon] Ḥārith?' (*ma anta yā Ḥārith*). Ḥārith replied: 'A believer, O Messenger of Allah' (*muʾminan yā Rasūl Allāh*). The Prophet ﷺ then said: 'Truly a believer?' (*muʾminun ḥaqqan*).

Ḥārith replied: 'Truly a believer' (*mu'minan ḥaqqan*). The Prophet ﷺ then said: 'For every truth there is a reality (*li-kull ḥaqq ḥaqīqa*), so what is the reality of this [your faith]?' (*fa-mā ḥaqīqat dhālika*).[194] This hadith can also serve a basis, on one possible interpretation, for asserting that both the logical order and the ontological order are not two separate orders.

Al-Qayṣarī (d. 751/1350), a disciple of ʿAbd al-Razzāq al-Qāshānī, states in the introduction to his commentary on Ibn ʿArabī's *Fuṣūṣ* that Adam ﷺ was appointed the *khalīfa* or vicegerent over the manifestation of His Names, namely, the world, *al-ʿālam* (the ordered world, as opposed to *dunyā,* the negative concept of the world). Each of the Divine Names governs a specific manifestation (*maẓharan khāṣṣan*), except for the All-encompassing Name (*al-ism al-jāmiʿ*), Allah, whose *maẓhar* (locus of manifestation) is the complete *maẓhar*. Similarly, Adam ﷺ is the comprehensive creation (*al-nashʾa al-jāmiʿa*), which inspires Qayṣarī to state, 'Glory be to Him who manifested Himself by His Essence for His Essence so He made to appear Adam ﷺ and made him vicegerent over the manifestation of His Names.'[195] Some commentators interpreted this as meaning that everything except Adam ﷺ in existence manifests through a specific name, which manifests in the extramental world (*yaẓharu fī al-ʿayn*) without the intermediation of a particular Name but through every Name and reality. In Adam ﷺ, Qayṣarī continues, every reality is recapitulated and furthermore concealed, so that Adam ﷺ would be the form of His complete Name, Allah, and the bearer of the secrets of the All-knowing, the Omniscient (*al-ʿālim al-aʿlam*), which is a proof of Him, and thus He comes to be known through him.[196] This is the overriding correspondence that cosmology reveals together with the teleological implications of creation.

Before examining the details of Ibn ʿArabī's encounter with Ibn Rushd, the epistemological context should be kept in mind. This is namely that for Ibn ʿArabī, every intellectual perception is deemed a necessary limitation of reality, a limitation which the heart alone can encompass in its entirety.

In chapter 15 of the *Futūḥāt al-Makkiyya*, Ibn ʿArabī relates a meeting between him and Ibn Rushd which took place in or around AH 577, five years or so before the philosopher's death and when Ibn ʿArabī was only seventeen years of age. The reason for the meeting came about due to the friendship that Ibn Rushd shared with Ibn ʿArabī's father and their mutual political affiliations at court. The fifteenth chapter of the *Futūḥāt* relating the meeting in question is entitled, 'On the knowledge of the Breaths (*fī ma'rifat al-anfās*) and the knowledge of their Poles (*wa-ma'rifat aqtābihā*) who are verified by them and their mysteries (*al-muḥaqqiqīna bi-hā wa-asrārihā*)'. The chapter deals with several topics regarding alchemy, the resurrection of the body, and the correspondence between man and cosmos. The key figure in the chapter is Mudāwī al-Kulūm (lit. the healer of injuries),[197] a name Ibn 'Arabī bestows on the Prophet Idrīs ﷺ and who is furthermore spoken of as the *qutb al-arwāḥ al-insāniyya* (the Pole of the human spirits)[198] and one of the twenty-five Poles who ruled over the communities that preceded Islam.[199] This figure we are told was given knowledge of medicine, and also of the First Age[200] (*al-dahr al-awwal*) from which all the ages are manifested. He was also given the knowledge of the science of alchemy, being the first to transmute base metal to gold, symbolizing the transmutation of the base soul into a realised soul. It is clear that this figure is also none other than the first Hermes, namely, the biblical Enoch. In the cosmology that Ibn 'Arabī expounds, the Prophet Idrīs ﷺ resides in the fourth celestial sphere, the sphere of the Sun. He is the *qutb* of the *awliyā'* (Pole of the Friends of God), who resides in the sphere that is at the heart of the World and the Heavens.[201]

Ibn 'Arabī states that the mysterious *fatā*, 'the spirit from whom I received what I have placed in this book',[202] spoke to him of a meeting that was convened by Mudāwī al-Kulūm wherein he gathered his companions at a village (*daskara*) in order to prepare them for his coming end. In this gathering, he tells them that they would need to fathom the symbolic allusions in his discourse in relation to themselves. He further admonishes his companions, warning them that this knowledge is not widely disseminated and counselling them that every type of knowledge has its adherents. He further states, among other matters, that this transitory world and the Garden share in 'brick and mason', and that there is a reciprocal relationship between them, so that one may consider the *Rawḍa* in the Prophet's ﷺ mosque as part of the Celestial Garden. Although the mass of believers are asked to accept this on faith, the people of unveiling (*ahl al-kashf*) have no need of this as they are able to actually see the continuity between this world and the Garden.[203] This naturally tallies with the observation by Ibn 'Arabī that one of the sciences given to the Prophet Idrīs ﷺ is that of the science of the macrocosm and microcosm, namely, the correspondences between the cosmos and its recapitulation, the human entity.

Some observations on the transportation of the philosopher's body from Marrakesh to Córdoba after his death in AH 595 follow the section in the chapter on the meeting with Ibn Rushd. Ibn 'Arabī recounts that when the casket (*tābūt*) enclosing the cadaver of the philosopher was loaded on a donkey, the books authored by the deceased were used to balance the load of the casket on the other side of the beast. One observer, Abū al-Ḥakam, a companion standing with Ibn 'Arabī, turned to him and Ibn Jubayr, the legal scholar also in attendance, and asked them whether they had noticed the reason for the balanced load, namely, the deceased's works, meaning his authored books. Whilst Ibn Jubayr, we are told, commends Abū al-Ḥakam for such a pithy observation, Ibn 'Arabī in contrast construes the incident as a warning and a caution to remember, seeing this 'balancing' as a spiritual fetter.

In any case the meeting between Ibn 'Arabī and Ibn Rushd forms the central part of the chapter in question in the *Futūḥāt*.

> One day I went to Córdoba and visited its *qāḍī*, Abū al-Walīd Ibn Rushd, who had been eager to meet me, because he had heard what God had accorded me in the course of my spiritual retreat (*khalwa*), and he had made no secret of his astonishment at what he had been told. For this reason, my father, who was one of his friends, sent me to his house one day on the pretext of an errand, but in reality to enable me to meet him. At that time I was still a beardless youth and my moustache had not yet fully grown. When I entered, he rose from his place and came across to meet me, receiving me with affection and consideration, and then embraced me and said: 'Yes,' and I in turn said: 'Yes.' His joy was great for my understanding him. Then I became aware of what had made him delighted in me, so I said to him: 'No.' Immediately, he became tense and his colour changed, and he seemed to doubt his own understanding. He then asked me: 'What kind of solution have you found for the matter through illumination (*kashf*) and divine inspiration (*al-fayḍ al-ilāhī*)? Is it identical with that which we receive from speculative reflection (*naẓar*)?' I replied: 'Yes and no. Between the yes and no, spirits take their flight from their matter and necks are separated from their bodies.' Ibn Rushd turned pale, I saw him begin to tremble; he murmured the ritual phrase

> 'There is no strength save in God' – for he had understood
> my allusion, and it is precisely the subject mentioned by this
> *quṭb imām,* that is, Mudāwī al-Kulūm.

There are two important issues to be ascertained here. The first is the specific subject matter of their agreement or disagreement, which we will leave to the side for our purposes. The second, which we will try to examine, concerns the modality of knowledge, since the philosopher brings this up specifically as a point of distinction between their two approaches; namely, the distinction and question of concurrence, or the lack of it, between knowledge arrived at by way of spiritual disclosure (*kashf*) and knowledge arrived at by way of reason (*'aql*). The question posed in effect is that of whether *kashf* can be said to yield a different type of knowledge, or on the other hand, whether the difference between it and knowledge arrived at by reason is one merely to do with the manner of acquisition.

The answer, we might contend, perhaps unsurprisingly, is yes and no. Knowledge is one, just as Reality is one in the Akbarian scheme, but is nevertheless subject to ontic multilateral and hierarchical levels. When one speaks of different knowledges, one is more properly referring to differing degrees of knowledge, rather than strictly different kinds. This goes to the heart of understanding the relationship between reason and *kashf,* and furthermore, the relationship between reason and that which is beyond reason, the *supra*-rational. When Ibn 'Arabī speaks of the knowledge of the saints (*awliyā'*) as *mā warā' ṭawr al-'aql,* beyond reason, he does not mean by this that such knowledge is irrational or *infra*-rational, but rather *supra*-rational. The difference being that the irrational essentially contravenes the rules of reason, and thus must inherently be unintelligible. We are, however, told in contradistinction that knowledge through *kashf* is intelligible to one of sound mind, and therefore cannot be said to contradict the rules of reason.[204] Such knowledge moreover cannot be reasoned to; one could say, the ladder of rational construction allowing the mind to arrive at such knowledge is missing. Such knowledge, though, once present in the mind, is acceptable to reason and thus can be assented to.[205]

This brings us to the examination of the category of that which is deemed impossible (*mustaḥīl*), and its relationship to what is deemed inconceivable (*mumtani' al-taṣawwur*). The impossible, in existing, is divided into impossible to exist *fī al-a'yān,* in extramental reality, and that which is *in strictu senso* impossible to exist. It was stated earlier in relation to inconceivability, that the inconceivable is impossible to exist, or else there would be two orders of being in contradiction, and the two orders cannot be in contradiction as being is one. Alternately, conception of a thing is not sufficient to determine possibility *de re*. This naturally depends on the meaning of the *real* impossible, as opposed to something which in itself is not impossible to exist but is considered to be so due to a subjective deficiency in its conception. Certain realms in the science of physics lend themselves readily to illustrate that many things may be inconceivable to the untrained mind, but nevertheless capable of existing or even do exist, such as electrons or quarks.

Prior to investigation of the possible, impossible, and necessary, following Ibn Sīnā, such an investigation necessarily demands or presumes the precedence of being. Primarily, nothing that exists is impossible, because the impossible necessarily lacks the condition for existence. In terms of conceivability, the consistency of a proposition, its definability, cannot be sufficient to establish impossibility *per se*. It is true that future contingencies are sometimes inconceivable, but it does not make those contingencies impossible. Therefore, where inconceivability is a relative matter relating to the capacity (*kayfiyya*) of a thinker or the circumstance that the thinker may find himself in, that is to say, a particular period in time with a particular understanding, such inconceivability would not be sufficient to imply a real impossibility. As was also said before, propositional inconsistency would bring about impossibility of definition, but not real impossibility. Similarly, careless and unsystematic thinking or inconsistency in thought would not bring about impossibility as such, but impossibility of thought, or at the very least clear thinking. This is important to keep in mind when the real inconceivable is deemed to be possible *de re*.

In *Mashāhid al-asrār*, when God interrogates him as to whom he considers himself to be, Ibn ʿArabī replies that he is apparent non-existence (*al-ʿadam al-ẓāhir*).

> The Real made me contemplate the light of existence as the star
> of direct vision (*ʿayān*) rose, and He asked me, 'Who are you?'
> I replied, 'Apparent non-existence (*al-ʿadam al-ẓāhir*).'
> Then He said to me, 'And how can non-existence change
> into existence (*wujūd*)? If you were not an existing [entity],

your existence would not be possible and real.'

I replied, 'That is why I said apparent non-existence, since hidden non-existence (*al-'adam al-bāṭin*) does not have real existence.[206]

Ibn 'Arabī is illustrating here the two types of non-existence, hidden non-existence that is impossible, 'real impossible', and relative non-existence that is apparent and possible. It is relative because it is apparent in God's knowledge in the *a'yān al-thābita* (affirmed potentialities), and then by His command is brought into contingent and apparent existence. The *'ayn thābit* according to Ibn 'Arabī is the reality of a thing in the Divine Knowledge, not in extramental reality, so to speak, in pre-eternal existence. It is in effect to be established in His knowledge but not manifested. The manifestation from being in the knowledge of God to relative contingency through the divine fiat *'kun'* ('be') is accomplished without any change to the *a'yān thābita,* as the realities do not change, *al-ḥaqā'iq lā tatabaddal.* Only the apparent non-existent is possible, while the hidden non-existent cannot be manifested.[207]

This passage is an example of prima facie contradictory assertions that in actuality present no contradiction due to ontological hierarchical modulation. This can be seen in the two propositions, Zayd exists, Zayd does not exist. Both can be said to be simultaneously true, one on an *i'tibārī* level, the other on a real level. At the level of *asbāb,* the sub-lunar world, Zayd exists; at another ontological resolution, Zayd does not exist, as only God exists. The two propositions, if we assume our interpretation, are referring to different ontological resolutions of existence.

In chapter 65[208] of the *Futūḥāt* on the Garden, Ibn 'Arabī confirms that there are two ways that lead to the knowledge of God, the highest and most worthy knowledge. The first is a necessary (*ḍarūrī*) knowledge which one finds in oneself through *kashf,* and which can neither be denied nor resisted. Furthermore, the one who receives this knowledge does not receive any proof (*dalīl*) by which it can be supported except what he possesses already. The view that the knowledge given by *kashf* is 'supplied' by the proof in his *mukāshafa* is rejected by Ibn 'Arabī, despite being cited as the opinion of the Ash'arī *mutakallim* in Fez Abū 'Abd Allāh Ibn al-Kattānī.[209] The latter's observation is deemed to be partially correct in accordance with his state, rather than with the truth of the matter according to Ibn 'Arabī. The rationale behind Ibn al-Kattānī's view was that if the matter unveiled required proof for it to be known, then the proof would be unveiled with the said knowledge in question. Ibn ʿArabī, on the other hand, held that some may find this knowledge in themselves without their being granted its proof nor the capacity to demonstrate it, since it remains unmediated in its process.

The second way for the knowledge of God that Ibn ʿArabī outlines is that which is acceded to through reflection (*fikr*) and investigation (*istidlāl*) by way of rational demonstration (*al-istidlāl bi-l-burhān al-ʿaqlī*). This second way is considered inferior to the first as it is based on proof (*dalīl*), because every rational proof can be subject to doubt and confusion, or alternatively, subject to strict intellectual discipline that may cast out such doubts. In his letter to Rāzī,[210] he counsels that it is incumbent on the *ʿāqil* to divest (*takhliya*) his heart of ratiocination if he wishes to reach the knowledge of God by way of *mushāhada* (witnessing). This impoverishment is necessarily demanded of the aspirant, as whatever does not have perfection (*kamāl*) except through that which is other than itself is poor, and this is the condition of everything other than God, for He is *al-Ghanī*.[211] This, however, does not amount to a denial of the powers of reasoning, nor a denial of the faculty of reason in preference to *kashf*, but a psychological reordering that permits one to place things in their rightful place. One could say that Ibn ʿArabī is warning that truth may be hidden by rational proofs, just as much as Being may be hidden by existents.

> Know that when the people of reflection attain the furthermost goal, their reflection takes them to the state of being deaf imitators. But the matter is too exalted for it to halt at reflection! So long as there is reflection, it will be impossible for one to repose and be at rest. The intellect has a limit at which it halts with respect to its reflective powers, for it has the quality of receiving [only] what God bestows upon it. Therefore, an intelligent person should expose himself to the divine breaths of generosity (*nafaḥāt al-jūd*) and not remain enslaved by the shackle of his rational consideration and learning (*kasb*), for he is liable to doubt (*shubha*) because of these.[212]

If the power of reasoning is indeed passive, in that the mind has the attribute of receptivity alone (*lahā ṣifat al-qabūl*) to what God bestows upon it, then the intellectual sciences at their highest level are a matter of inspiratory gift (*wahb*) rather than *kasb*. In the *Muqaddima* to the *Futūḥāt*, Ibn ʿArabī states categorically that the intellect has limits at which it ceases to function as a thinking tool, but not in its receptive capacity to divine inspiration. He further continues that with regard to something that may be considered rationally impossible, the case may not be impossible in relation to God, just as what the intellect may consider possible may nevertheless be impossible in relation to God.[213] This essentially is the distinction between the real and the relative impossible.

The issue of opposites (*al-aḍdād*) is one that was mentioned at the beginning of this section and which one frequently comes across in Ibn ʿArabī's writings, but also in other traditions, as in the Madhyamaka tradition of Buddhism, one that Graham Priest has seen fit to use as grist for his own dialetheistic mill.[214] The Names of God are an example of opposites that some have interpreted as representing contradictories, such as *al-ẓāhir wa-l-bāṭin*, the Apparent and the Hidden, *al-awwal wa-l-ākhir*, the First and the Last.

Contradictions, however, do not admit of degrees; contraries do. The Names of God are not opposites that contradict each other, they are opposites that are united in the Name of Allah, *al-ism al-jāmiʿ*. If they were contradictory, apart from the absurd theological implications this would have, then they would not be able to be both true at the same time, and we know them to be both true, because God tells us so. They are furthermore not contradictory as they are in breach of the unity of predicates, *waḥdat al-maḥmūl*; for example, *ẓāhir wa-bāṭin*. He is *al-ẓāhir* to Himself and remains so, and He is *al-bāṭin* for His creation and remains so. They are, strictly speaking, not contraries, as contraries cannot both be true, and here the Names are both true. They may be considered subcontraries as this categorization permits them to be both true, but the truth of one cannot be inferred from the other in subcontraries as shown above, and here the Names can be inferred due to God's perfection requiring each of the pair. As can be seen, mere opposition is not sufficient to amount to a contradiction, itself the most perfect form of opposition. Qayṣarī also states in his *Sharḥ* that between two contrary Names (*ismayn mutaqābilayn*) exists a Name that possesses both aspects (*isman dhā wajhayn*) of the two contraries, and born out of them (*mutawallidan minhumā*).[215] This Name, we are told, stands as a *barzakh* between the two respective Names, the two polarizations, which affirms the point that the two Names may be inferred from each other.

Qayṣarī makes mention of the above context when discussing *wujūd* in his *Muqaddima*.[216] He states that through Being, opposites (*ḍiddan*) or contraries are realized, and identicals are sustained (*yataqawwamu al-mithlān*). He continues:

It is [*wujūd* in the sense of Being] that manifests itself in the form of contraries, and in others, and this manifestation [in the form of contraries] necessitates a union of contradictories (*al-jamʿ bayn al-naqīḍayn*). Since each part of the contradiction negates the other, the difference between the two parts is a conceptual construct (*bi-iʿtibār al-ʿaql*). Nonetheless all aspects are united in Being (*wujūd*); so that manifestation (*al-ẓuhūr*) and that which is inwardly hidden (*al-buṭūn*) and all the ontological attributes (*al-ṣifāt al-wujūdiyya*) in opposition are dissolved in Being (*mustahlika fī ʿayn al-wujūd*), and there is no differentiation except conceptually (*fa-lā mughāyara illā fī iʿtibār al-ʿaql*).

The use of the terms *al-jamʿ bayn al-naqīḍayn* is not in the strict sense of contradiction but is used in a *majāz* sense to mean contraries or opposites which are mutually exclusive. What Qayṣarī intends above is that the PNC is a logical principle when we come to discuss propositional contradictions, but, ontologically speaking, there are no contradictions *per se*, as things simply *are*, contradiction being a relation we deduce, a mental relation. As a principle of being, the matter as shown above becomes of an entirely different order. In metaphysical judgement, one can only separate what is really separated in reality; for example, being and non-being. It is from this separation, one being from another being, that one is able to discern the meaning of being. In *taṣawwur*, the intellect is concerned with one aspect of being and not its relation to any other being. In metaphysics, the intellect seeks to know the ontological nature of reality and the existence of things.

This brings us to the discussion of the passage cited earlier in the *Taʿlīqāt* where Ibn Sīnā stated that it was impossible for one to know the reality of things. He further states in the *Taʿlīqāt* the reason for this:

Man can never apprehend the reality of the thing precisely because the basis of his knowledge of things begins with sense perception (*al-ḥiss*). After this, he distinguishes intellectually between the similar (*al-mutashābihāt*) and the completely distinct (*al-mutabāyināt*), so that he thus comes to know intellectually some of its concomitants, acts, effects, and properties and, from this, arrives at a kind of general summary knowledge of it that has not been verified (*ghayr muḥaqqaqa*) with those of its concomitants which he does not know except the obvious ones. He may know it for the most part, but it is not necessary that he know all its concomitants. If he knew the reality of the thing, though, and descends from a true knowledge down towards its concomitants and properties, he would know as a matter of course these concomitants and properties in their entirety. His way of knowing, though, is the reverse of what it ought to be.[217]

Ibn Sīnā is essentially saying that the form seized by the intellect is not a perfect likeness of the essence of an object. In other words, the intellect cannot grasp in a single intuition the respective form's sum of intelligibility, hence the possibility of intellectual error. Rather, the intellect arrives at the inner nature of a thing through the instrumentality of the senses, which do not penetrate beyond external accidents and in any case are not seized completely, or all at the same time. The intellect thus may be said to be gradually perfecting its understanding through various syntheses, that is to say, judgements, and judgements can be wrong. So, we can say that it is only through *taṣawwur* that we accede to knowledge, but concepts do not amount to knowledge *per se*. There is only knowledge when some form of judgement has been made about them, the process of judgement being the process of synthesis. At the level of *taṣawwur*, therefore, one cannot strictly speak of intellectual error. This possibility only belongs to the domain of judgement.

One can also add that in preceding passages, we had examined the operation of the estimative faculty (or better still, the cogitative faculty, *al-quwwa al-wahmiyya*) stating that this faculty prepares, assisted by memory and the imagination, the assembly of the common sense for the operation of the Active Intellect. That is to say, that together with the product of the senses mediated by the common sense, it brings together memories and associations by which even external experience may be interpreted, for the operation of thought. Thus, through the possible errors of the preparation of this faculty, thought may be unable to attain truth.

The last line of the above-quoted passage from the *Taʿlīqāt* mirrors the methodology utilized by figures such as Ṣadr al-Dīn al-Qūnawī, providing a resolution to the limitations imposed by the rational faculty in eliciting knowledge of the realities, as it were, 'from below'. In his exchange of correspondence with Ṭūsī, Qūnawī, after quoting the above passage from Ibn Sīnā, states that the basis of knowledge for the people of *dhawq* (taste) is the knowledge of the Real (*mabda' maʿrifatihim maʿrifat al-Ḥaqq*). This knowledge is by way of God and not their own powers and intellects. If they know God, Qūnawī continues, through God (*ʿarafū al-Ḥaqq bi-l-Ḥaqq*), they may then know themselves through God. It is impossible, therefore, according to Qūnawī, for one to know the reality of a thing, if one does not know God.²¹⁸ How does one, then, attain to the knowledge of God? This question cannot be treated here in this paper as it requires a fulsome answer, which happily Qūnawī provides. Moreover, it also provides a fulsome solution to the so-called problem of knowledge that plagues the corridors and halls of modern philosophy.

Afterword

It is the task of revelation to provide definable and recognizable references that can be brought into human understanding. Logic is given the role of providing in us an eternal order reflective of the order of creation, a role that bestows upon it, therefore, a certain sacrality. The Kantian conceptualist contention, now often encountered, establishes the basis for the de-ontologization of logic, since it creates a split between second intentions and first intentions, ensuring that reality has no input into the workings of the mind. Secondary intelligibles, however, are based on first intelligibles – things that exist – and thus they are ontologically dependent and reflective of that order.²¹⁹

The loss of cognitive order is synonymous with the loss of the order of the sciences. It is this latter order that provides us with the intellectual hierarchies necessary to understand the workings of first principles and all that flows from them. The role of metaphysics, as has been argued, is one that needs to be re-established so that the limitations inherent in every science may be safeguarded and observed. The reassertion of an effective division of the sciences provides a panoramic grid that then permits the scholar to situate the properties of his contentions and theories, allowing for a thorough analysis of theoretical thought to be carried out in the light of principles. Principial thought, in this context, is organized thought that provides for cosmological realism as well as metaphysical realism at the same time.

It is also apt to recapitulate that much of modern philosophy rests on assumptions and postulates that have not been demonstrated, and largely cannot be demonstrated. In this case, they become articles of belief, much like any denigrated faith-knowledge in the secularist mindset. This brings us to the brief mention of belief. One of the singular dangers facing the Islamic knowledge framework is the increasing rationalization of the doctrines of the faith. As the environment in the Islamic world becomes more and more tempered by technological structures in the built environment that have little to do with the human scale, there is correspondingly an increased demand for instrumentalist proofs of the articles of faith. This carries with it a danger, if it is correctly understood, because that which underpins traditional beliefs in the intellectual order is metaphysics, whose principles cannot be demonstrated nor reasoned to, as its truths impose themselves upon us. These truths cannot be reasoned to because they form the basis of reasoning itself. Similarly, when it comes to the starting point of logical thinking, the self-evident premise can neither be proven nor demonstrated, as it is the basis or starting point of any demonstration. The danger lies in effectively attempting to rationalize sublime truths, and by rationalizing them, destroying them.

All metaphysical cognition is a form of a meta-sensual vision (*shuhūd*) at its highest level, and consequently true cognition can never be 'blind'. The act of cognitive assent is thus the activation of the will once this vision has been gifted. Metaphysical cognition, therefore, is the highest conviction possible that one may have, more than any dialectical process may deliver when arriving at a reasoned conclusion. A conclusion may be reasoned out of, much in the manner of how it was reasoned into. True metaphysical thought, however, cannot be reasoned in or out of. Naturally, reasoned conclusions are always needed, but then what we are speaking of is a matter of degree. When it comes to first principles like the PNC, as was stated above, the principles are seen to be in operation and thus must be assented to, not demonstrated. Their effects may be demonstrated, but not the principles themselves.

Much of the revival of *kalām* in recent times has paid scant attention to this point of supra-rationality and more perhaps towards intellectual arm-twisting techniques, traditional or otherwise, that attempt to go head-to-head with modern contentious philosophies. In a world increasingly drowning in the noise of discourse and debate, a more subtle and empowering approach might be best served by reanimating hearts to the recognition once again of the order of metaphysics and the manner in which it flows and directs our intellectual consciousness. Cosmology is metaphysics writ large around us and in us. It is in this sense that traditional knowledge, its culture, and its systems of transmission are rooted in reality, and thus its principles can never be subject to change. In more than one sense, one can say that traditional intellectual knowledge need hardly ever be proved but rather discovered or unveiled in its natural order. ❧

Notes

1. Scientific knowledge in this instance does not refer to the natural sciences but to a body of knowledge that is ordered in line with an external hierarchy, its place in the division of the sciences, and an internal hierarchy, the architectural composition of its subject matter and scope of interest in line with ordering principles.

2. The term 'tradition' (and 'traditional') is used throughout this paper not as a mere term of historiography, and thus of diachronic or even synchronic significance alone. It is admitted that tradition is a clumsy word, much abused, and over-prescriptive in the historical and even Roman Catholic context. By its use, nevertheless, the aim is to signify the understanding of an intellectual and social order founded on Islamic cosmological and ontological principles, an order that necessarily premises itself on the foundations of an agreed-upon *ʿaqīda* established from the Revelation by the scholars of *Ahl al-Sunna wa-l-Jamāʿa*. By ontological and cosmological is meant the understanding that this world is a mirror of the macrocosmos, and that existence and existents are hierarchically and divinely posited in the created world in accordance with the Divine Knowledge, and thus inscribed with divine meaning. When something is said to be traditional, that is to say, recognizing and acting upon this signification, its effects might be observed and analysed both diachronically and synchronically.

3. We see this clearly in Ibn Sīnā's formulation of certitude in his treatment of the syllogisms, where certitude is calibrated by psychological receptivity and inclination.

4. See Karim Lahham, *Muhammad Shahrur's 'Cargo Cult': A Meditation on His Underlying Conceptual Framework,* Tabah Papers Series 4 (Abu Dhabi: Tabah Foundation, 2012).

5. 'Dés lors *connaître c'est fabriquer,* nous ne connaissons que ce que nous faisons. Voilà l'axiome secret qui domine toute la philosophie spéculative de Kant. Et si connaître c'est fabriquer, les choses elles-mêmes ne sont pas connaissables, puisque nous ne le faisons pas, le seul objet de notre connaissance, c'est l'objet que nous faisons grâce à nos formes *a priori,* – un monde de phénomènes dont la loi, l'unité, la structure constitutive et la régulation viennent toutes de notre esprit.' See Jacques Maritain, *Réflexions sur l'intelligence et sur sa vie propre* (Paris: Nouvelle Librairie Nationale, 1926), 34–35.

6. ʿAllāma Quṭb al-Dīn Maḥmūd ibn Masʿūd Kāzirūnī al-Shīrāzī, *Sharḥ-i Ḥikmat al-Ishrāq Suhrawardī* (Tehran: Institute of Islamic Studies, 2001), 32.

7. See Julius Weinberg, *Nicolaus of Autrecourt: A Study in 14th-Century Thought* (Princeton, NJ: Princeton University Press, 1948); Georges de Lagarde, *La naissance de l'esprit laïque au déclin du moyen âge*, 6 vols (Paris: Presses Universitaires de France, 1934–46); Paul Vignaux, *Nominalisme au XIVe siècle* (Paris: Librairie J. Vrin, Conférence Albert-Le-Grand, 1948); Stephen Gaukroger, *The Emergence of a Scientific Culture: Science and the Shaping of Modernity, 1210–1685* (Oxford: Oxford University Press, 2006), chapters 3–5.

8. Paul Nwyia, ed., *Ibn ʿAtāʾAllāh (m. 709/1309) et la naissance de la confrérie shādilite, Édition critique et traduction des Ḥikam* (Beirut: Dar El-Machreq Éditeurs, 1971), no. 27, 98–99; Ibn ʿAṭāʾillāh, *Sufi Aphorisms (Kitāb al-ḥikam)*, trans. Victor Danner (Leiden: Brill, 1973), no. 29, 28 (translation slightly modified).

9. See Dimitri Gutas, 'Avicenna and After: The Development of Paraphilosophy: A History of Science Approach', in *Islamic Philosophy from the 12th to the 14th Century*, ed. Abdelkader al-Ghouz (Bonn: Bonn University Press, V & R Unipress, 2018), 19–71, at 51.

10. Heidrun Eichner, *The Post-Avicennian Philosophical Tradition and Islamic Orthodoxy: Philosophical and Theological Summae in Context* (Halle: Habilitationsschrift, 2009), 420, quoted in Gutas, 'Avicenna and After', 52. Figures such as Abharī, Lawkarī, and Kātibī may have treated the sciences encyclopaedically on the lines of Ibn Sīnā, but their treatment is a cursory one.

11. Gutas, 'Avicenna and After', 52.

12. Ibid., 56.

13. It is this dependence that Avicenna institutes in his *Ilāhiyyāt* of the *Shifāʾ*, in contradistinction to Aristotle on this point.

14. That is to say, the derivation of a judgement from a notion or another judgement. Aristotle considered the axioms as the laws of the formation of inferences.

15. John Stuart Mill, *A System of Logic, Ratiocinative and Inductive: Being a Connected View of the Principles of Evidence, and the Methods of Scientific Investigation*, vol. 1 (Cambridge: Cambridge University Press, 2012), 244–45.

16. Jonathan Barnes, *Aristotle's Posterior Analytics*, Clarendon Aristotle Series (Oxford: Clarendon Press, 1975), chapter 3, 5–7, A2 72b–73b. Bekker numbering is retained throughout this paper for Aristotelian texts. Translations are for the most part based on Barnes; text editions based on Ross.

17. Method is a way to arrive at a doctrine. It may be defined as the order to be observed in a series of actions so that a definite goal or purpose may be attained. Whenever a definite goal is to be attained by a series of actions,

then method is important, to build a house, bake a cake, etc. Methods are neither true nor false; they are good or bad. A good method is one by which the desired goal can be attained effectively. A bad method is one where the desired goal cannot be attained at all or with great difficulty.

18. Emerich Coreth, *Metaphysics* (New York: Herder and Herder, 1968), 31–44.

19. Richard McKeon, 'Aristotle's Conception of the Development and Nature of the Scientific Method', *Journal of the History of Ideas* 8, no. 1 (January 1947): 3–44, at 20.

20. Shams al-Dīn al-Samarqandī, *Qisṭās al-afkār fī taḥqīq al-asrār* (Ankara: Türkiye Yazma Eserler Kurumu Başkanlığı, 2014), 491–93. For *metabásis*, see *An. Post.*, I.7.75a38; for subalternation, *An. Post.*, I.7.75b15.

21. *An. Post.*, I.2.71b16–25.

22. Literally, lacking a middle term.

23. *An. Post.*, I.2.71b20–22.

24. Ibid., I.2.71b26–29.

25. Richard D. McKirahan, *Principles and Proofs: Aristotle's Theory of Demonstrative Science* (Princeton, NJ: Princeton University Press, 1992), 24–25.

26. *An. Post.*, I.2.72a5–8.

27. Ibid., I.3.72b7–15. On the exclusion of circularity from demonstrative science, for example, Aristotle states: 'For all practical thinking there are limits – as such thinking is for the sake of something else, whereas all speculative thinking in like manner is limited by ideas and every idea is either a definition or a demonstration. But demonstrations begin from principles, and have as their term a conclusion or an inference – but even if they are never brought to an end they do not come round again to their starting point; they continue to take a new middle term or extreme and go straight forward, whereas the circular movement returns once more to the starting point. Definitions too are all finite.' *De Anima*, I.3.

28. *An. Post.*, I.10.76a37–10.76b3.

29. Ibid., I.28.87a39.

30. McKirahan, *Principles and Proofs*, 51.

31. 'One cannot, therefore, prove anything by crossing from another genus – e.g. something geometrical by arithmetic ... Now the things on which the demonstrations depend may be the same; but of things whose genus is different – such as arithmetic and geometry – one cannot apply arithmetical demonstrations to the accidentals of magnitudes, unless magnitudes are numbers ... Arithmetical demonstrations always include the genus about which the demonstration is, and so also do the others; hence it is necessary for the genus to be the same, either *simpliciter* or in some respect, if the demonstration is going to cross. That it is impossible otherwise is clear; for it is necessary for the extreme and the middle terms to come from the same genus. For if they do belong themselves, they will be accidentals.' *An. Post.*, I.7.75a38–75b12.

32. Ibid., II.17.99a22–23. Aristotle states at I.12.77b5–15: 'We should not, therefore, ask each scientist every question, nor should he answer everything he is asked about anything, but only those determined by the scope of this science [in this case geometry]. If one argues in this way with a geometer as geometer it is evident that one will do so correctly, if one proves something from these things; but otherwise, not correctly. And it is clear that one does not refute the geometer either, except incidentally; so that one should not argue about geometry among non-geometers – for the man who argues badly will escape notice. And the same goes for the other sciences too.'

33. Ibn Sīnā mirrors this determination in his *Kitāb al-burhān*, Ibn Sīnā, *al-Shifāʾ: al-Burhān*, Ed. Ibrāhīm Madkūr and Abū al-ʿIla ʿAfīfī (Cairo: al-Maṭbaʿa al-Amiriyya, 1956), II.155, where he states that each science has a subject matter, principles, and questions (*masāʾil*). This will be discussed further below.

34. *An. Post.*, I.9.75b38–76a8.

35. Ibid., I.7.75b8–9.

36. Ibid., I.9.76a22–25.

37. Respectively, ibid., I.9.76a10, 22–25; and I.12.77b1–2. See the discussion in Richard McKirahan, 'Aristotle's Subordinate Sciences', *The British Journal for the History of Science* 11, no. 3 (1978): 197–220.

38. The term was coined by the Paduan Aristotelian logician Giacomo Zabarella (d. 1589), who stated that there were two parts to a subject: the first being the material part, *res considerata*, which formed the object of the investigation and which could be common to several sciences. The second was the formal part, *modus considerandi*, which was the perspective through which this object is considered, and which was proper to the particular science. See Marco Sgarbi, *The Aristotelian Tradition and the Rise of British Empiricism: Logic and Epistemology in the British Isles (1570–1689)* (Dordrecht: Springer, 2013), 57–58. McKirahan, 'Aristotle's Subordinate Sciences', 202, refers to what the sciences have in common as *modus considerandi*. Equally Steven J. Livesey, *Theology and Science in the Fourteenth Century: Three Questions on the Unity and Subalternation of the Sciences from John of Reading's Commentary on the Sentences*, Introduction and Critical Edition (Leiden: E. J. Brill, 1989), 24.

39. McKirahan, 'Aristotle's Subordinate Sciences', 202.

40. *Burhān inna.*

41. *Burhān lima.*

42. *An. Post.*, I.13.78b32–79a7.

43. Ibid., I.13.79a3–7. What Aristotle is saying is that the geometer may not know necessarily the particular facts in optics, but if he were to be presented with them, would be able to furnish an explanation for them in the science of geometry.

44. Ibid., I.13.79a3.

45. Ibid., I.9.76a11.

46. It should suffice to point to the application of the categorical syllogism to the Qur'an in Ghazālī's *al-Qisṭās al-mustaqīm*, and Najm al-Din al-Ṭūfī's *'Alam al-jadhal fī 'ilm al-jadal*. The 'Aristotelian' nature of Ghazālī's *Maḥakk al-naẓar fī al-manṭiq* and his *Mi'yār al-'ilm* is, needless to say, also self-evident. As the Imam states in the prefaces to the *Tahāfut*, there is no opposition to the philosophers' logic nor their natural philosophy, but rather the disagreement hinges on their false metaphysics. See Abū Ḥāmid al-Ghazālī, *Tahāfut al-falāsifa* (Beirut: al-Maṭbaʿa al-Kāthūlīkiyya, 1345/1927), 44–45; Michael Marmura, 'Ghazālī and Demonstrative Science', in *Probing in Islamic Philosophy: Studies in the Philosophies of Ibn Sīnā, al-Ghazālī and Other Major Muslim Thinkers* (Albany, NY: State University of New York Press, 2005), 231–60.

47. See Bilal Ibrahim, 'Freeing Philosophy from Metaphysics: Fakhr al-Din al-Razi's Philosophical Approach to the Study of Natural Phenomena' (PhD diss., McGill University, 2013); Bilal Ibrahim, 'Fakhr ad-Dīn ar-Rāzī, Ibn al-Haytham and Aristotelian Science: Essentialism versus Phenomenalism in Post-classical Islamic Thought', *Oriens* 41 (2013): 379–431; Amos Bertolacci, 'The "Ontologization" of Logic: Metaphysical Themes in Avicenna's Reworking of the Organon', in *Methods and Methodologies: Aristotelian Logic East and West, 500–1500*, ed. Margaret Cameron and John Marenbon (Leiden: Brill, 2011), 27–52.

48. Ibn Sīnā, *al-Madkhal (Isagoge)*, ed. M. Khudayrī, G. Qanawātī, and A.F. Ahwānī, revised by I. Madkūr (Cairo: al-Maṭbaʿa al-Amiriyya, 1371/1952), bk.1, ch.1, 12–15.

49. Ibn Sīnā, *Burhān*, II.7, on classification and subalternation; II.8, on *metabasis*.

50. Ibn Sīnā, *al-Najāt* (Cairo: Muḥyī al-Dīn Ṣabrī al-Kurdī, 1356/1938), 72–75.

51. Ibn Sīnā, *al-Ishārāt wa-l-tanbīhāt, 'ilm al-manṭiq, al-nahj al-tāsi'*, faṣl 3–4, ed. M. al-Zirāʿī (Qom: Bustān-e ketāb-e, 1381/1961), 168–70.

52. In Ibn Sīnā, *Tis' rasā'il fī al-ḥikma wa-l-ṭabī'iyyāt* (Istanbul: 1298/1880), 105–6.

53. What we mean here are natural bodies, that is to say, bodies that have extension in all three dimensions. These natural bodies can consist of simple bodies, or plants with a capacity for growth and decrease, or animals which have in addition to the qualities of plants, locomotion and perception.

54. For example, Ibn Sīnā, *Burhān*, II.6, is a paraphrase of *An. Post.*, I.7.75a39–75b2. For a concordance of the chapters of *Burhān* with the *Posterior Analytics*, see Riccardo Strobino, 'Avicenna on the Indemonstrability of Definition', *Documenti e studi sulla tradizione filosofica medievale* 21 (2010): 113–63.

55. Ibn Sīnā, *Burhān*, II.7.165-66. This notion is also mirrored in Ibn Sīnā, *Ilāhiyyāt*, I.2.12, where metaphysics is distinguished but nevertheless shown to have some shared aspects with dialectical and sophistical arguments.

56. Ibn Sīnā, *Burhān*, II.7.166.7–9. See translation in Amos Bertolacci, *The Reception of Aristotle's Metaphysics in Avicenna's Kitāb al Shifā'* (Leiden: Brill, 2006), 233-234.
57. Ibid., II.6.155.
58. Ibn Sīnā, *al-Burhān*, I.1.51.
59. Ibn Sīnā, *Burhān*, I.1.51; see also Deborah Black, 'Certitude, Justification and Principles of Knowledge in Avicenna's Epistemology', in *Interpreting Avicenna: Critical Essays,* ed. Peter Adamson (Cambridge: Cambridge University Press, 2013), 122.
60. Ibn Sīnā, *Burhān,* I.1.53.
61. Ibn Sīnā, *al-Shifā': al-Ilāhiyyāt,* intro. and rev. I. Madkūr, ed. G. Qanawātī and S. Zāyid (Cairo: Wizārat al-Thaqāfa wa-l-Irshād al-Qawmī, 1960), I.2.15, I.3.23. All translations of passages in the *Ilāhiyyāt* will use or rely on Marmura's translation in Avicenna, *The Metaphysics of the Healing: A Parallel English-Arabic Text,* Islamic Translation Series, trans., intro., and annot. Michael E. Marmura (Provo, UT: Brigham Young University Press, 2005).
62. Ibn Sīnā, *Ilāhiyyāt,* I.2, I.3.
63. This hierarchical structure pointedly ensured a largely stable and principial approach to reality, which we would contend gave much of the pre-industrial Islamic world its lucid and coherent world-view that resisted the impulse to trespass the limits of nature. Interestingly, Bertolacci recognizes this concomitance, albeit from a different perspective altogether:

    'This well-structured system of sciences, culminating in metaphysics as the crowning discipline, is remarkable for coherence and solidity; but has certain disadvantages. For, if the dependence of all the other disciplines on metaphysics guarantees the system a strong "focal" unity, it also prevents the single sciences from proceeding and developing autonomously. This probably explains why the many concrete observations present in Avicenna's philosophy of nature – and in all the subsequent authors adopting his same classification of sciences – did not and could not evolve into a fully accomplished empirical approach to reality. Only when, in modern times, metaphysics ceased to regulate and "control" from above the other sciences, a so-called "scientific revolution" within the system of knowledge became possible.' Bertolacci, *The Reception,* 266.
64. Ibn Sīnā, *Ilāhiyyāt,* I.1.5.
65. Ibid., I.8.54, see Bertolacci, 222. Ibn Sīnā clarifies further on: 'In addition to all this, the investigation of the principles of conception and definition is not itself definition and conception; nor is the investigation of the principles of demonstration (*mabādi' al-burhān*) itself a demonstration (*burhān*) for the two distinct investigations become one [and the same].' I.8.54, see Marmura translation.
66. Ibn Sīnā, *Burhān,* I.1.53.
67. Ibid., II.6.155.4–12 (trans. Bertolacci, 134).

68. Ibid., II.7.166.
69. See 'The Epistemological Dimension' section below.
70. Ibn Sīnā, *Kitāb al-taʻlīqāt,* ed. Badawī (Qom: Maktab al-Iʻlām al-Islāmī fī al-Ḥawza al-ʻIlmiyya, 1404), 34. I have relied on the translation found in Anthony Shaker, *Thinking in the Language of Reality* (USA: Xlibris, 2015), 112.
71. Ibid., 82.
72. Ibn Sīnā, *Burhān,* I.6.30.10–12, 77.3–5.
73. Ibid., I.3.57.
74. Ibn Sīnā, *Kitāb al-najāt* (Beirut: Manshūrāt Dār al-Āfāq al-Jadīda, 1985), 108. I have made use of the translations, with slight modifications, in Asad Q. Ahmed, *Avicenna's Deliverance: Logic* (Karachi: Oxford University Press, 2011), 105.
75. ʻAllāma Ḥillī, *al-Jawhar al-naḍīd: Sharḥ Manṭiq al-tajrīd* (Qom: Intishārāt Bidār, 1433), 328–29. See also Ibn Sīnā, *al-Ishārāt wa-l-tanbīhāt* (Qom: Nashr al-Balāgha, 1375), I.299–300.
76. Ḥillī, *al-Jawhar al-naḍīd,* 329.
77. Ibid., 328.
78. This is the syllogism that shows the truth of the conclusion by proving the falsity of its contradictory. See, for example, Suhrawardī, *The Philosophy of Illumination,* ed. and trans. John Walbridge and Hossein Ziai (Provo, UT: Brigham Young University Press, 1999), 26.
79. See for example, ʻAbd al-ʻAzīz Ibn Bazīza al-Tūnisī, *al-Isʻād fī sharḥ al-Irshād* (Kuwait: Dār al-Ḍiyāʼ, 2014), 118. This may also be considered as belonging to the categories of the *maḥsūsāt,* sense-based knowledge, or *mujarrabāt,* experiment-based knowledge, that are both considered part of the category of *ḍarūrī* knowledge. See ʻAlī ibn Muḥammad al-Jurjānī, *Sharḥ al-Mawāqif* (Beirut: Dār al-Kutub al-ʻIlmiyya, 2012), II.38–39.
80. Jurjānī, *Sharḥ al-Mawāqif,* I.131.
81. Ibid., 131–32.
82. Ibid., II.39–40.
83. Ibid., 40.
84. Ibid. See also Quṭb al-Dīn al-Rāzī's commentary on *Sharḥ al-Shamsiyya,* where the commentator takes the view that the distinction between *mujarrabāt* and *ḥadsiyyāt* lies in the requirement of repeated observations for the former and none for the latter, a position held by al-Laknawī in *Sharḥ Baḥr al-ʻulūm* following Ṭūsī's position in *Sharḥ al-Ishārāt.* This is significantly different from Jurjānī, as we have seen above, who does not absolve the *ḥadsiyyāt* from this requirement. See Quṭb al-Dīn al-Rāzī, *Taḥrīr al-qawāʻid al-manṭiqiyya fī sharḥ al-Risāla al-shamsiyya* (Beirut: Muʼassasat al-Tārīkh al-ʻArabī, 2011), 459; Abū al-ʻAyyāsh al-Laknawī, *Sharḥ Baḥr al-ʻulūm* (Kuwait: Dār al-Ḍiyāʼ, 2012), 561–62.

85. See ʿAṭṭār's commentary on Zakariyya al-Anṣārī, *al-Maṭlaʿ Sharḥ Īsāghūjī* (Kuwait: Dār al-Ḍiyāʾ, 2017), 145. Fakhr al-Dīn al-Rāzī's position is a well-known exception to this, in that he declared *taṣawwur* to be always *badīhī* and never capable of being *naẓarī*.

86. Jurjānī, *Sharḥ al-Mawāqif*, II.77: 'Badāhat al-taṣawwur ṣifa khārija ʿanhu fa-jāza an takūna maṭlūbatan lahu bi-l-burhān.'

87. Ibid., I.69.

88. This remains unedited. Ms. İstanbul Süleymaniye Kütüphanesi Hacı Selim Ağa 723, folio 44b ff.

89. Nāṣir al-Dīn al-Bayḍāwī, *Tawāliʿ al-anwār* (Qom: Intishārāt Rāʾid, 1393), I.42–43.

90. See the Iṣfahānī commentary below (note 91).

91. Najm al-Dīn al-Kātibī al-Qazwīnī, *Ḥikmat al-ʿayn* (Istanbul: Türkiye Yazma Eserler Kurumu Başkanlığı, 2016), 55, 57.

92. Shams al-Dīn al-Iṣfahānī, *Tasdīd al-qawāʿid fī sharḥ Tajrīd al-ʿaqāʾid* (Kuwait: Dār al-Ḍiyāʾ, 2012), 186–92.

93. ʿAllāma Ḥillī, *Kashf al-murād fī sharḥ Tajrīd al-iʿtiqād* (Qom: Muʾassasat al-Nashr al-Islāmī, 1432), 29–33.

94. The missing and unexamined argument in Iṣfahānī consists of the first way set out in the *Mulakhkhaṣ*. It states that the knowledge of one's existence is a part of one's existence, and the knowledge of the part precedes knowledge of the whole (*al-ʿilm bi-l-juzʾ sābiq ʿalā al-ʿilm bi-l-kull*), and that which precedes the necessary must be necessary *a fortiori*, and knowledge is one as a whole, therefore absolute knowledge is necessary. Iṣfahānī, *Tasdīd al-qawāʿid*, 186n5. See also Jurjānī, *Sharḥ al-Mawāqif*, I.69.

95. In Iṣfahānī's recension.

96. Iṣfahānī, *Tasdīd al-qawāʿid*, 187.

97. Goichon suitably refers to this as an *éclair de compréhension*. See A.-M. Goichon, *La distinction de l'essence et de l'existence d'après Ibn Sīnā* (Paris: Desclée de Brouwer, 1937), 308.

98. See Rāzī, *Taḥrīr al-qawāʿid*, 459–60. See also Ibn Sīnā, *Burhān*, III.9.259.

99. Ibn Sīnā, *al-Mubāḥathāt*, ed. Muḥsin Bidarfar (Qom: Intishārāt Bidār, 1413), 107.

100. Fakhr al-Dīn al-Rāzī, *Sharḥ al-Ishārāt* (Tehran: Anjuman-i Āṣār va Mafākhir-i Farhangī, 1384), II.269.

101. Ibid.

102. Ibid., II.417.

103. Ibid., II.271; trans. Shams Inati, *Ibn Sīnā's Remarks and Admonitions: Physics and Metaphysics* (New York: Columbia University Press, 2014), 103.

104. Rāzī, *Sharḥ al-Ishārāt*, II.271–73.

105. Ibid., II.214.

106. Ibid., II.216; Inati's translation here is a little abstruse, perhaps incomprehensible, 'To apprehend a thing is to have its reality represented to him

who apprehends such that it is observed by that with which he apprehends.' Inati, *Remarks and Admonitions,* 98.

107. Rāzī, *Sharḥ al-Ishārāt,* II.236; Inati, *Remarks and Admonitions,* 99.

108. In accordance with Suhrawardī, see his *Kitāb al-lamaḥāt,* ed. Emile Maalouf (Beirut: Dār al-Nahār, 1969), 115.

109. Ibid.

110. See Ibn Sīnā, *Kitāb al-nafs,* ed. Fazlur Rahman, *Avicenna's De Anima: Being the Psychological Part of Kitāb al-Shifā'* (London: Oxford University Press, 1959), IV.2.175, translated from the latter by Deborah Black, 'Rational Imagination: Avicenna on the Cogitative Power', in *Philosophical Psychology in Medieval Arabic and Latin Aristotelianism,* ed. Jorg Tellkamp and Luis Xavier Lopez Farjeat (Paris: Vrin, 2013), 59–81. There is some scholarly dispute as to whether the imaginative faculty can receive forms, not just from the depository provided through the common sense, but also from the celestial intelligences. This also concerns whether its powers of division and composition can also be directed not just by the human intellect or estimative faculty but also by a higher celestial power.

111. This is the principal faculty for judgements in animals; see *Kitāb al-nafs,* IV.1.167.

112. I have followed Carla Di Martino in referring to *maʿānī* as intentions; see *Ratio Particularis: Doctrines des sens internes d'Avicenne à Thomas d'Aquin* (Paris: Vrin, 2008), 24.

113. *Kitāb al-nafs,* I.5.43. See also Di Martino, *Ratio Particularis,* 25.

114. Di Martino, *Ratio Particularis,* 27.

115. Ibn Sīnā, *Kitāb al-nafs,* II.2.58–59; Di Martino, *Ratio Particularis,* 27.

116. Di Martino, *Ratio Particularis,* 30; see also *Kitāb al-nafs,* IV.1.163–64.

117. Ibn Sīnā, *Kitāb al-nafs,* II.2.58.

118. Ibid., II.2.59.

119. Ibid., II.2.60.

120. Ibid., I.5.49.

121. I have chosen 'articulate' rather than 'rational' to avoid the misconceptions and prejudicial limitations surrounding the latter in Western thought.

122. Suhrawardī, *Lamaḥāt,* 120.

123. Dimitri Gutas, *Avicenna and the Aristotelian Tradition,* 2nd ed. (Leiden: Brill, 2014), 182–83. See also his 'Avicenna: The Metaphysics of the Rational Soul', *The Muslim World* 102 (2012): 417–25, at 420–21.

124. See ʿAllāma Ḥillī, *al-Jawhar al-naḍīd,* 328-329.

125. See Martin X. Moleski, SJ, for a useful definition of retortion in, 'Retortion: The Method and Metaphysics of Gaston Isaye', *International Philosophical Quarterly* 27 (1977): 59–83. 'Retortion is essentially a process of recognizing inconsistency in a philosophical position. It results in the judgement that no person could adopt such a position without becoming involved in a kind of self-contradiction. This places it in the genre of *ad hominem* argu-

ments, although "the *Homo* in question is every *Homo*, every human being." An argument which is subject to retortion is rejected because no one can adopt it consistently, not simply because the argument is inconsistent with a particular person's beliefs. Since it is implicitly concerned with all men, retortion can lead us to a universally valid statement about the nature of man and the nature of being.'

126. So *mushāhadāt, maḥsūsāt, mujarrabāt, ḥadsiyyāt,* and *mutawātirāt.* See above for an explanation of their typology.

127. Ibn Sīnā, *Burhān,* I.4.63–64.

128. Ibid., 64.

129. Ibn Sīnā, *Najāt,* 99; (Ahmed) 90; and Dimitri Gutas, 'The Empiricism of Avicenna', *Oriens* 40 (2012): 391–436, at 408–9. Ahmed translates *fiṭra* as 'primary intelligence'. Gutas refers to it as 'the natural operation of the mind', which is more appropriate in our opinion. I have preferred to leave the word untranslated. In his notes to the passage, Ahmed states that *fiṭra* is a natural and sound disposition for understanding, thus a form of intelligence. The point here is that both the intellect, directed towards intelligibles, and the faculty of estimation, directed towards sensibles, have their own spheres of natural understanding. See Ahmed, 161-162.

130. Ibn Sīnā, *Najāt,* 98.

131. Ibid., 99.

132. See below.

133. Ibn Sīnā, *al-Shifāʾ: al-Manṭiq – al-Maqūlāt,* ed. G. Qanawātī, M. Khudayrī, A.F. Ahwānī, and S. Zāyid (Cairo: Wizārat al-Thaqāfa wa-l-Irshād al-Qawmī, 1959), 241. I have relied on Allan Bäck's translation: Avicenna, *Al-Maqūlāt: Commentary on Aristotle's Categories,* Analytica Liber Conversus Series, trans. and intro. Allan Bäck (Munich: Philosophia Verlag GmbH., 2016), 335.

134. Ibid., 241.

135. Ibid., 243.

136. Naṣīr al-Dīn al-Ṭūsī, *Talkhīṣ al-Muḥaṣṣal,* ed. ʿAbd Allāh Nūrānī (Tehran: Dānishgāh-i Makgīl, bā hamkārī-i Dānishgāh-i Ṭihrān, 1359), 27; Jurjānī, *Sharḥ al-Mawāqif,* I.154–55.

137. Ṭūsī, *Talkhīṣ,* 27.

138. This is an assent or dissent, which is firm merely for practical reasons, because otherwise life would be impossible. So, for example, we are practically certain a cook will not poison the food in a restaurant.

139. Ṭūsī, *Talkhīṣ,* 29.

140. See Joep Lameer, 'غير المعلوم يمتنع الحكم عليه (*Ghayr al-maʿlūm yamtaniʿ al-ḥukm ʿalayhi*): An Exploratory Anthology of a False Paradox in Medieval Islamic Philosophy', *Oriens* 42, no. 3–4 (2014): 397–453.

141. Ṭūsī, *Talkhīṣ,* 29.

142. Jurjāni, *Sharḥ al-Mawāqif,* I.158–59.

143. I am grateful for reading the relevant passages of the *Talkhīṣ* referred to here under the kind direction of Dr Wahid Amin. Any errors in understanding are mine alone.

144. Ṭūsī, *Talkhīṣ*, 29.

145. This also reminds one of the saying of Abū Bakr al-Ṣiddīq, often quoted by Shaykh al-Akbar: '*Al-ʿajz ʿan dark al-idrāk idrāk*' ('Incapacity to attain perception is perception'). See, for example, Ibn ʿArabī, *al-Futūḥāt al-Makkīyya* (Beirut: Dār Ṣādir, n.d.), II.619.

146. Lameer, 'Exploratory Anthology', 411–12.

147. Ibn Sīnā, *Ilāhiyyāt*, I.8; (Marmura) 39.

148. Ibn Sīnā, *Ilāhiyyāt*, I.8.53.6; (Marmura) 42.

149. Contrariety is defined as the propositions that are never true together but might be false together, but the cases of truth and falsity are determined exactly. It is less strong than contradiction because A and E are opposed only in two matters in the square of opposition. See Saloua Chatti, 'Logical Oppositions in Arabic Logic: Avicenna and Averroes', in *Around and Beyond the Square of Opposition*, Studies in Universal Logic series, ed. Jean-Yves Béziau and Dale Jacquette (Basel: Springer, 2012), 21–40, at 25.

150. '"*Tadākhul*" is *not* synonymous with the traditional word "Subalternation" since it does not have the same linguistic meaning. While "Subalternation" derives from the Latin words "*alter*" which means "other" and "*sub*" which means "under" and evokes the notion of dependence (upon the other) and thus implication, the Arabic word comes from the root "*dakhala*" which is a verb meaning "to enter", the other verb, which is closer to the word used, is "*tadākhala*" and means "to enter into each other". The ideas involved then are the ideas of inclusion and of the relation between the whole and the part: the part is included into the whole, therefore what is true of the whole is true of the part.' Ibid., 26–27.

151. That is to say, 'if P, then Q', but also, 'if Q, then P'. An exclusive disjunction would be 'if P, then not Q', but also, 'if Q, then not P'. If you combine the two, P and Q, then they are in contradiction, 'either P or Q'. If P and Q are incompatible but not exhaustive, they are contrary, 'P or Q or neither'. If they are exhaustive but not incompatible, they are subcontrary, 'P or Q or both'.

152. Saʿd al-Dīn al-Taftāzānī, *Tahdhīb al-manṭiq wa-l-kalām* (Kuwait: Dār al-Ḍiyāʾ, 2017), 200.

153. Ibn Sīnā, *al-Shifāʾ: al-Manṭiq – al-ʿIbāra*, ed. Maḥmūd al-Khuḍarī (Cairo: al-Hayʾa al-Miṣriyya al-ʿĀmma li-l-Nashr wa-l-Tawzīʿ, 1970), 54.

154. Luqmān al-Kurdī, *Taqwiyat al-ṭālib al-muqaddis fī sharḥ Miftāḥ al-shaykh al-mudarris fī ʿilm al-manṭiq* (Kirkuk, Iraq: Maktabat Amīn, 2018), 156–57; Ḥillī, *al-Jawhar al-naḍīd*, 124–28.

155. The square as a figure together with the terms, subalternates and subcontraries, are not to be found in Aristotle's *De Interpretatione*, 7.

156. See James Quin, 'God and the Intelligibility of Being', *Philosophical Studies* 15 (1966): 211–14.

157. Representing the positive and negative aspects of this intuition.

158. *De Interpretatione*, chapter 9.

159. Ahad Faramarz Qaramaleki, *12 Treatises on Liar Paradox in Shiraz School* (Tehran: Iranian Institute of Philosophy, 2007).

160. See Saʿd al-Dīn al-Taftāzānī, *Sharḥ al-Maqāṣid*, vol. 4, ed. ʿAbd al-Raḥmān ʿUmayra (Beirut: ʿĀlam al-Kutub, 1998), 286–87.

161. See, for a full treatment of the matter, David Sanson and Ahmed Alwishah, 'Al-Taftāzānī on the Liar Paradox', in *Oxford Studies in Medieval Philosophy*, vol. 4, ed. Robert Pasnau (Oxford: Oxford University Press, 2014), 100–124.

162. See John Neville Keynes, *Studies and Exercises in Formal Logic* (London: Macmillan and Co., 1906), 458.

163. This was originally published in Russian in the *Journal of the Ministry of People's Education*, New Series, August 1912, part 40, 207–46. It was subsequently translated in 2003 as Nicolai Vasiliev, 'Imaginary (Non-Aristotelian) Logic', *Logique & Analyse* 182 (2003): 127–63.

164. Ibid., 127.

165. The modern mathematician, it should be added, understands axioms and postulates none too differently when they distinguish them. A postulate is a proposition about the elements of the given science, while an axiom is any proposition from another science which is necessary in the given science.

166. Vasiliev, 'Imaginary (Non-Aristotelian) Logic', 134.

167. Ibid., 135.

168. Ibid.

169. Ibid.

170. Ibid., 136.

171. Ibid., 136–37.

172. Ibid., 138.

173. Ibid.

174. Immanuel Kant, *Critique of Pure Reason,* trans. Norman Kemp Smith (London: Macmillan, 1933), 190 (A151/B190).

175. Immanuel Kant, *Versuch, den Begriff der negativen Grössen in die Weltweisheit einzuführen* [Attempt to introduce the concept of negative magnitudes into philosophy] (Königsberg: 1763). See Immanuel Kant, *Theoretical Philosophy 1755–1770* (Cambridge: Cambridge University Press, 1992), 211.

176. See Marco Giovanelli, *Reality and Negation – Kant's Principle of Anticipations of Perception: An Investigation of Its Impact on the Post-Kantian Debate* (Dordrecht: Springer, 2011), 41–42.

177. Kant, *Theoretical Philosophy,* 212.

178. Kant, *Critique of Pure Reason,* 189–90 (A151/B190–B191).

179. Friedrich Ueberweg, *System of Logic and History of Logical Doctrines*, trans. Thomas Lindsay (London: Longmans, Green and Co., 1871), 236.
180. Kant, *Critique of Pure Reason*, 190 (A151/B190).
181. Ibid.
182. Kant, *Critique of Pure Reason*, 191 (A153/B192).
183. Ibid.
184. See Mustafa Styer's paper on definition published in the Classification of the Sciences Project Tabah Papers Series.
185. See above.
186. Shams al-Dīn al-Samarqandī, *Science of the Cosmos and the Soul: ʿIlm al-āfāq wa-l-anfus*, ed. Gholamreza Dadkhah (Costa Mesa, CA: Mazda Publishers, 2014), 95.
187. One who is in full possession of his mental faculties.
188. Samarqandī, *Science of the Cosmos and the Soul*, 95.
189. *Idh mā min shayʾ illā wa-yūjad fīhi āyāt kamālihi wa-ʿalāmāt jalālihi.*
190. This is in line with the saying '*Man ʿarafa nafsahu fa-qad ʿarafa rabbahu*' ('He who knows himself, knows his Lord'), sometimes attributed as a hadith, though more likely a *khabar* of Yahyā ibn Muʿādh al-Rāzī.
191. See Ibn ʿAjība, *al-Baḥr al-madīd*, vol. 5, ed. Bassām Muḥammad Barūd (Abu Dhabi: n.d.), 575. Ibn ʿAjība, somewhat confusingly, refers to Baqlī as Wartajabī, identified as the same author by Alan Godlas.
192. Ibn ʿArabī, *Fuṣūṣ al-ḥikam*, ed. Sayyid Niẓām al-Dīn Aḥmad al-Ḥusaynī al-Laknawī (Cairo: Maktabat Miṣr, 2005), 9.
193. al-Rāghib al-Iṣfahānī, *Mufradāt alfāẓ al-Qurʾān* (Damascus: Dār al-Qalam, 1997), 247. See also ʿAbd Allāh al-Ṣiddīq al-Ghumārī, *Mawsuʿāt al-ʿAllāma al-Muḥaddith al-Mutafannin ʿAbd Allāh al-Ṣiddīq al-Ghumārī*, vol. 11 (Cairo: 1438), 331–32.
194. The hadith continues: 'He said: "I have abstained from the world and kept vigil during my nights and remained thirsty during my days. It is as if I am witnessing the Throne of my Lord (*ʿarsh rabbī ʿazza wa-jalla*), and it is as if I see the people of Paradise visiting each other (*yatazāwarūna fīhā*), and it as if I can hear the wailing of the people of Hell." And the Prophet ﷺ said: "He is a believer whose heart God has illuminated (*muʾmin nawwara Allāh qalbahu*)."'
195. '*Fa-subḥān alladhī tajallā bi-dhātihi li-dhātihi fa-aẓhara Ādam wa-stakhlafahu ʿalā maẓāhir asmāʾihi.*' Sharaf al-Dīn Dāwūd al-Qayṣarī, *Sharḥ Fuṣūṣ al-ḥikam*, 2 vols, ed. Ḥasan Zādeh ʿĀmulī (Beirut: Manshūrāt, n.d.), I.13.
196. Ibid.
197. Injuries caused by *hawā* (caprice).
198. Ibn ʿArabī, *Futūḥāt*, II.437.
199. See Michel Chodkiewicz, 'Toward Reading the *Futūḥāt Makkiyya*', in *Ibn ʿArabi: The Meccan Revelations; Selected Texts of the Futūḥāt al-Makkiya* (Lahore: Suhail Academy, 2005), II.35.

200. This is in effect the first temporal cycle, the age of the Seven Sleepers in the cave. When the Quraysh, before the Hijra, consulted the Jews of Medina about the Prophet ﷺ, much of the *tafsīr* literature in relation to *al-Kahf* states that they suggested that certain questions be put to him, so that he might be exposed. The first question they suggested to ask him was as to the whereabouts and circumstances of the young men who disappeared during the first temporal cycle (*fī al-dahr al-awwal*).

201. Ibn ʿArabī, *Futūḥāt*, II.437.

202. The book being his *Futūḥāt*.

203. Chodkiewicz, 'Toward Reading the *Futūḥāt Makkiyya*', II.36.

204. Ibn ʿArabī, *Futūḥāt*, I.261.

205. I am indebted in this section to ʿAbd al-Bāqī Miftāḥ's commentary on the meeting of Ibn Rushd and Shaykh al-Akbar in his *Buḥūth ḥawl kutub wa-mafāhim al-Shaykh al-Akbar Muḥyī al-Dīn Ibn ʿArabī* (Beirut: Dār al-Kutub al-ʿIlmiyya, 2011), 145–66.

206. Sitt ʿAjam bint al-Nafīs, *Sharḥ al-Mashāhid al-qudsiyya li-takmīl dāʾirat al-khatm al-mawṣūf bi-l-walāya al-Muḥammadiyya: Muḥammad Ibn ʿArabī*, ed. Bakrī ʿAlāʾ al-Dīn and Suʿād al-Ḥakīm (Damascus: Institut Francais du Proche-Orient, 2004) 25–38; translation used from Ibn ʿArabī, *Contemplation of the Holy Mysteries*, trans. Pablo Beneito Arias and Jane Clark (Oxford: Anqa Publishing, 2000), 23.

207. ʿAbd al-Bāqī Miftāḥ, *al-Sharḥ al-Qurʾānī li-Kitāb Mashāhid al-asrār li-l-Shaykh al-Akbar Muḥyī al-Dīn Ibn ʿArabī* (Beirut: Dār al-Kutub al-ʿIlmiyya, 2010), 73.

208. Ibn ʿArabī, *Futūḥāt*, I.319.

209. This figure, also known as Abū ʿAbd Allāh al-Fandalāwī (d. AH 597), features in various disputes with Ibn ʿArabī, and is one of the figures cited in Ibn al-Zayyāt, *al-Tashawwuf ilā rijāl al-taṣawwuf wa-akhbār Abī al-ʿAbbās al-Sabtī* (Rabat: Manshūrāt Kulliyyāt al-Adab wa-l-ʿUlūm al-Insāniyya, 1984), 335–37, cited in Claude Addas, *Quest for the Red Sulphur* (Cambridge: Quinta Essentia, 1993), 135 ff.

210. See *Risāla ilā al-Imām al-Rāzī* in *Rasāʾil Ibn al-ʿArabī* (Hyderabad, Deccan: Dāʾirat al-Maʿārif al-Osmāniyya, 1948), 2; Ibn ʿArabī, 'Epître adressée à l'imâm Fakhru-d-Dîn ar-Râzî, trans. Michel Vâlsan, *Études Traditionnelles*, no. 366–67 (July–August and September–October 1961): 242; see also Mohammed Rustom, 'Ibn ʿArabi's Letter to Fakhr al-Dīn al-Rāzī: A Study and Translation', *Journal of Islamic Studies* 25, no. 2 (2014): 113–37.

211. 'O Mankind! You are needful of God; and He is the Self-sufficient, the Praised' (Q35:15).

212. *Risāla ilā al-Imām al-Rāzī*, 3. I have used the translation in Rustom, 'Ibn ʿArabi's Letter', 131–32.

213. Ibn ʿArabī, *Futūḥāt*, I.41.

214. See Graham Priest, *The Fifth Corner of Four: An Essay on Buddhist Meta-physics and the Catuskoti* (Oxford: Oxford University Press, 2018). This work attempts to look at the conundrums of the Tetralemma in the work of Nagarjuna and its attendant non-Aristotelian implication to traditional logic.

215. Qayṣarī, *Sharḥ Fuṣūṣ al-ḥikam*, 71.

216. Ibid., 26.

217. Ibn Sīnā, *Kitāb al-taʿliqāt*, ed. ʿAbd al-Raḥmān al-Badawī (Qom: Maktab al-Iʿlām al-Islāmī, 1404), 82.

218. See Gudrun Schubert, ed., *al-Murāsalāt bayn Ṣadr al-Dīn al-Qūnawī wa-Naṣīr al-Dīn al-Ṭūṣī* (Beirut: Steiner Verlag, 1995), 52–53.

219. Incidentally, the system of knowledge we are speaking of is never thus a closed system and hence the lack of any discussion of Gödel's theorems in this paper, as they do not apply.

Bibliography

Adamson, Peter, ed. *Interpreting Avicenna: Critical Essays*. Cambridge: Cambridge University Press, 2013.

Addas, Claude. *Quest for the Red Sulphur*. Cambridge: Quinta Essentia, 1993.

Ahmed, Asad Q. *Avicenna's Deliverance: Logic*. Karachi: Oxford University Press, 2011.

al-Anṣārī, Zakariyya. *al-Maṭlaʿ Sharḥ Īsāghūjī*. Kuwait: Dār al-Ḍiyāʾ, 2017.

Avicenna. *The Metaphysics of the Healing: A Parallel English-Arabic Text*. Islamic Translation Series. Translated, introduced, and annotated by Michael E. Marmura. Provo, UT: Brigham Young University Press, 2005.

———. *al-Maqūlāt: Commentary on Aristotle's Categories*. Analytica Liber Conversus Series. Translated and introduced by Allan Bäck. Munich: Philosophia Verlag GmbH., 2016.

Barnes, Jonathan. *Aristotle's Posterior Analytics*. Clarendon Aristotle Series. Oxford: Clarendon Press, 1975.

———, ed. *The Complete Works of Aristotle: The Revised Oxford Translation*. Bollingen Series LXXI. Princeton, NJ: Princeton University Press, 1984.

al-Bayḍāwī, Nāṣir al-Dīn. *Tawāliʿ al-anwār*. Qom: Intishārāt Rāʾid, 1393.

Bertolacci, Amos. *The Reception of Aristotle's Metaphysics in Avicenna's Kitāb al Shifāʾ*. Leiden: Brill, 2006.

Béziau, Jean-Yves, and Dale Jacquette, eds. *Around and Beyond the Square of Opposition*. Studies in Universal Logic. Basel: Springer, 2012.

Bint al-Nafīs, Sitt ʿAjam. *Sharḥ al-Mashāhid al-qudsiyya li-takmīl dāʾirat al-khatm al-mawṣūf bi-l-walāya al-Muḥammadiyya: Muḥammad Ibn ʿArabī*. Edited by Bakrī ʿAlāʾ al-Dīn and Suʿād al-Ḥakīm. Damascus: Institut Francais du Proche-Orient, 2004.

Cameron, Margaret, and John Marenbon, eds. *Methods and Methodologies: Aristotelian Logic East and West, 500–1500*. Leiden: Brill, 2011.

Chodkiewicz, Michel, ed. *Ibn ʿArabi: The Meccan Revelations; Selected Texts of the Futūḥāt al-Makkiya*. Lahore: Suhail Academy, 2005.

Coreth, Emerich. *Metaphysics*. New York: Herder and Herder, 1968.

De Lagarde, Georges. *La naissance de l'esprit laïque au déclin du moyen âge*. 6 vols. Paris: Presses Universitaires de France, 1934–46.

Di Martino, Carla. *Ratio Particularis: Doctrines des sens internes d'Avicenne à Thomas d'Aquin*. Paris: Vrin, 2008.

Eichner, Heidrun. *The Post-Avicennian Philosophical Tradition and Islamic Orthodoxy: Philosophical and Theological Summae in Context*. Halle: Habilitationsschrift, 2009.

Gaukroger, Stephen. *The Emergence of a Scientific Culture: Science and the Shaping of Modernity 1210–1685*. Oxford: Oxford University Press, 2006.

al-Ghazālī, Abū Ḥāmid. *Tahāfut al-falāsifa*. Beirut: al-Maṭbaʿa al-Kāthūlīkiyya, 1345AH/1927CE.

al-Ghouz, Abdelkader, ed. *Islamic Philosophy from the 12th to the 14th Century*. Bonn: Bonn University Press, V & R Unipress, 2018.

al-Ghumārī, ʿAbd Allāh al-Ṣiddīq. *Mawsuʿāt al-ʿAllāma al-Muḥaddith al-Mutafannin ʿAbd Allāh al-Ṣiddīq al-Ghumārī*. Cairo: 1438.

Giovanelli, Marco. *Reality and Negation – Kant's Principle of Anticipations of Perception: An Investigation of Its Impact on the Post-Kantian Debate*. Dordrecht: Springer, 2011.

Goichon, A.-M. *La distinction de l'essence et de l'existence d'après Ibn Sīnā*. Paris: Desclée de Brouwer, 1937.

Gutas, Dimitri. 'Avicenna: The Metaphysics of the Rational Soul'. *The Muslim World* 102 (2012): 417–25.

———. 'The Empiricism of Avicenna'. *Oriens* 40 (2012): 391–436.

———. *Avicenna and the Aristotelian Tradition*. 2nd ed. Leiden: Brill, 2014.

Ḥillī, ʿAllāma. *Kashf al-murād fī sharḥ Tajrīd al-iʿtiqād*. Qom: Muʾassasat al-Nashr al-Islāmī, 1432.

———. *al-Qawāʿid al-jaliyya fī sharḥ al-Risāla al-shamsiyya*. Edited by Fāris Ḥassūn Tabrīziyān. Qom: Muʾassasat al-Nashr al-Islāmī, 1432.

———. *al-Jawhar al-naḍīd: Sharḥ Manṭiq al-tajrīd*. Qom: Intishārāt Bidār, 1433.

Ibn ʿAjība. *al-Baḥr al-madīd*. 5 vols. Edited by Bassām Muḥammad Barūd. Abu Dhabi: n.d.

Ibn ʿArabī. *al-Futūḥāt al-Makkiyya*. Beirut: Dār Ṣādir, n.d.

———. *Risāla ilā al-Imām al-Rāzī* in *Rasāʾil Ibn al-ʿArabī*. Hyderabad, Deccan: Dāʾirat al-Maʿārif al-Osmāniyya, 1948.

———. 'Epître adressée à l'imâm Fakhru-d-Dîn ar-Râzî'. Translated by Michel Vâlsan. *Études Traditionnelles*, no. 366–67 (July–August and September–October 1961): 242–53.

———. *Contemplation of the Holy Mysteries*. Translated by Pablo Beneito Arias and Jane Clark. Oxford: Anqa Publishing, 2000.

———. *Fuṣūṣ al-ḥikam*. Edited by Sayyid Niẓām al-Dīn Aḥmad al-Ḥusaynī al-Laknawī. Cairo: Maktabat Miṣr, 2005.

Ibn ʿAṭāʾillāh. *Sufi Aphorisms (Kitāb al-ḥikam)*. Translated by Victor Danner. Leiden: Brill, 1973.

Ibn Sīnā. *Tisʿ rasāʾil fī al-ḥikma wa-l-ṭabīʿiyyāt*. Istanbul: 1298/1880.

———. *al-Najāt*. Cairo: Muḥyī al-Dīn Ṣabrī al-Kurdī, 1356/1938.

———. *al-Shifāʾ: al-Mantiq – al-Madkhal (Isagoge)*. Edited by M. Khudayrī, G. Qanawātī, and A.F. Ahwānī. Revised by I. Madkūr. Cairo: al-Maṭbaʿa al-Amiriyya, 1371/1952.

———. *al-Ishārāt wa-l-tanbīhāt*. Qom: Nashr al-Balāgha, 1375.

———. *al-Shifāʾ: al-Mantiq – al-Burhān*. Edited by A. Afifi. Cairo: al-Maṭbaʿa al-Amiriyya, 1375/1956.

———. *al-Shifāʾ: al-Manṭiq – al-Maqūlāt*. Edited by G. Qanawātī, M. Khudayrī, A. F. Ahwānī, and S. Zāyid. Cairo: Wizārat al-Thaqāfa wa-l-Irshād al-Qawmī, 1959.

———. *al-Shifāʾ: al-Ṭabīʿiyyāt – Kitāb al-nafs*. See Fazlur Rahman, ed. *Avicenna's De Anima*, 1959.

———. *al-Shifāʾ: al-Ilāhiyyāt*. Introduced and revised by I. Madkūr. Edited by G. Qanawātī and S. Zāyid. Cairo: Wizārat al-Thaqāfa wa-l-Irshād al-Qawmī, 1960.

———. *al-Ishārāt wa-l-tanbīhāt*. Edited by M. al-Zirāʿī. Qom: Bustān-e ketāb-e, 1381/1961.

———. *al-Shifāʾ: al-Ṭabīʿiyyāt – Kitāb al-nafs*. Edited by Jūrj Qanawātī and Saʿīd Zāyid. Cairo: al-Hayʾa al-Miṣriyya al-ʿĀmma li-l-Nashr wa-l-Tawzīʿ, 1975.

———. *Kitāb al-taʿlīqāt*. Edited by Badawī. Qom: Maktab al-Iʿlām al-Islāmī fī al-Ḥawza al-ʿIlmiyya, 1404.

———. *al-Mubāḥathāt*. Edited by Muḥsin Bidarfar. Qom: Intishārāt Bidār, 1413.

Ibn al-Zayyāt. *al-Tashawwuf ilā rijāl al-taṣawwuf wa-akhbār Abī al-ʿAbbās al-Sabtī*. Rabat: Manshūrāt Kulliyyāt al-Adab wa-l-ʿUlūm al-Insāniyya, 1984.

Ibrahim, Bilal. 'Fakhr ad-Dīn ar-Rāzī, Ibn al-Haytham and Aristotelian Science: Essentialism versus Phenomenalism in Post-classical Islamic Thought'. *Oriens* 41 (2013): 379–431.

———. 'Freeing Philosophy from Metaphysics: Fakhr al-Din al-Razi's Philosophical Approach to the Study of Natural Phenomena'. PhD diss., McGill University, 2013.

Inati, Shams. *Ibn Sīnā's Remarks and Admonitions: Physics and Metaphysics*. New York: Columbia University Press, 2014.

al-Iṣfahānī, al-Rāghib. *Mufradāt alfāẓ al-Qur'ān*. Damascus: Dār al-Qalam, 1997.

al-Iṣfahānī, Shams al-Dīn. *Tasdīd al-qawāʿid fī sharḥ Tajrīd al-ʿaqāʾid*. Kuwait: Dār al-Ḍiyāʾ, 2012.

al-Jurjānī, ʿAlī ibn Muḥammad. *Sharḥ al-Mawāqif*. Beirut: Dār al-Kutub al-ʿIlmiyya, 2012.

Kant, Immanuel. *Critique of Pure Reason*. Translated by Norman Kemp Smith. London: Macmillan, 1933.

———. *Theoretical Philosophy 1755–1770*. Cambridge: Cambridge University Press, 1992.

Keynes, John Neville. *Studies and Exercises in Formal Logic*. London: Macmillan and Co., 1906.

al-Kurdī, Luqmān. *Taqwiyat al-ṭālib al-muqaddis fī sharḥ Miftāḥ al-shaykh al-mudarris fī ʿilm al-manṭiq*. Kirkuk, Iraq: Maktabat Amīn, 2018.

Lahham, Karim. *Muḥammad Shaḥrūr's 'Cargo Cult': A meditation on his underlying conceptual framework*. Tabah Papers Series 4. Abu Dhabi, UAE: Tabah Foundation, 2012.

al-Laknawī, Abū al-ʿAyyāsh. *Sharḥ Baḥr al-ʿulūm*. Kuwait: Dār al-Ḍiyāʾ, 2012.

Lameer, Joep. 'غير المعلوم يمتنع الحكم عليه (*Ghayr al-maʿlūm yamtaniʿ al-ḥukm ʿalayhi*): An Exploratory Anthology of a False Paradox in Medieval Islamic Philosophy'. *Oriens* 42, no. 3–4 (2014): 397–453.

Livesey, Steven J. *Theology and Science in the Fourteenth Century: Three Questions on the Unity and Subalternation of the Sciences from John of Reading's Commentary on the Sentences*. Introduction and Critical Edition. Leiden: E. J. Brill, 1989.

Maritain, Jacques. *Réflexions sur l'intelligence et sur sa vie propre*. Paris: Nouvelle Librairie Nationale, 1926.

Marmura, Michael. *Probing in Islamic Philosophy: Studies in the Philosophies of Ibn Sīnā, al-Ghazālī and Other Major Muslim Thinkers.* Albany, NY: State University of New York Press, 2005.

McKeon, Richard. 'Aristotle's Conception of the Development and Nature of the Scientific Method'. *Journal of the History of Ideas* 8, no. 1 (January 1947): 3–44.

McKirahan, Richard D. 'Aristotle's Subordinate Sciences'. *The British Journal for the History of Science* 11, no. 3 (1978): 197–220.

———. *Principles and Proofs: Aristotle's Theory of Demonstrative Science.* Princeton, NJ: Princeton University Press, 1992.

Miftāḥ, 'Abd al-Bāqī. *al-Sharḥ al-Qur'ānī li-Kitāb Mashāhid al-asrār li-l-Shaykh al-Akbar Muḥyī al-Dīn Ibn 'Arabī.* Beirut: Dār al-Kutub al-'Ilmiyya, 2010.

———. *Buḥūth ḥawl kutub wa-mafāhim al-Shaykh al-Akbar Muḥyī al-Dīn Ibn 'Arabī.* Beirut: Dār al-Kutub al-'Ilmiyya, 2011.

Mill, John Stuart. *A System of Logic, Ratiocinative and Inductive: Being a Connected View of the Principles of Evidence, and the Methods of Scientific Investigation.* Vol. 1. Cambridge: Cambridge University Press, 2012.

Moleski, Martin X., SJ, 'Retortion: The Method and Metaphysics of Gaston Isaye'. *International Philosophical Quarterly* 27 (1977): 59–83.

Nwyia, Paul, ed. *Ibn 'Atā'Allāh (m. 709/1309) et la naissance de la confrérie shādilite, Édition critique et traduction des Ḥikam.* Beirut: Dar El-Machreq Éditeurs, 1971.

Pasnau, Robert. *Oxford Studies in Medieval Philosophy.* Vol. 4. Oxford: Oxford University Press, 2014.

Priest, Graham. *The Fifth Corner of Four: An Essay on Buddhist Metaphysics and the Catuskoti.* Oxford: Oxford University Press, 2018.

Qaramaleki, Ahad Faramarz. *12 Treatises on Liar Paradox in Shiraz School.* Tehran: Iranian Institute of Philosophy, 2007.

al-Qayṣarī, Dāwūd. *Sharḥ Fuṣūṣ al-ḥikam.* 2 vols. Edited by Ḥasan Zādeh 'Āmulī. Beirut: Manshūrāt, n.d.

al-Qazwīnī, Najm al-Dīn al-Kātibī. *Ḥikmat al-'ayn.* Istanbul: Türkiye Yazma Eserler Kurumu Başkanlığı, 2016.

Quin, James. 'God and the Intelligibility of Being'. *Philosophical Studies* 15 (1966): 211–14.

Rahman, Fazlur, ed. *Avicenna's De Anima: Being the Psychological Part of Kitāb al-Shifā'.* London: Oxford University Press, 1959.

al-Rāzī, Fakhr al-Dīn. *Sharḥ al-Ishārāt*. Tehran: Anjuman-i Āṣār va Mafākhir-i Farhangī, 1384.

al-Rāzī, Quṭb al-Dīn. *Taḥrīr al-qawāʿid al-manṭiqiyya fī sharḥ al-Risāla al-shamsiyya*. Beirut: Muʾassasat al-Tārīkh al-ʿArabī, 2011.

Rustom, Mohammed. 'Ibn ʿArabi's Letter to Fakhr al-Dīn al-Rāzī: A Study and Translation'. *Journal of Islamic Studies* 25, no. 2 (2014): 113–37.

al-Samarqandī, Shams al-Dīn. *Qisṭās al-afkār fī taḥqīq al-asrār*. Ankara: Türkiye Yazma Eserler Kurumu Başkanlığı, 2014.

———. *Science of the Cosmos and the Soul: ʿIlm al-āfāq wa-l-anfus*. Edited by Gholamreza Dadkhah. Costa Mesa, CA: Mazda Publishers, 2014.

Schubert, Gudrun, ed. *al-Murāsalāt bayn Ṣadr al-Dīn al-Qūnawī wa-Naṣīr al-Dīn al-Ṭūsī*. Beirut: Steiner Verlag, 1995.

Sgarbi, Marco. *The Aristotelian Tradition and the Rise of British Empiricism: Logic and Epistemology in the British Isles (1570–1689)*. Dordrecht: Springer, 2013.

Shaker, Anthony. *Thinking in the Language of Reality*. USA: Xlibris, 2015.

al-Shīrāzī, ʿAllāma Quṭb al-Dīn Maḥmūd ibn Masʿūd Kāzirūnī. *Sharḥ-i Ḥikmat al-Ishrāq Suhrawardī*. Tehran: Institute of Islamic Studies, 2001.

Strobino, Riccardo. 'Avicenna on the Indemonstrability of Definition'. *Documenti e studi sulla tradizione filosofica medievale* 21 (2010): 113–63.

Suhrawardī, Shihāb al-Dīn. *Kitāb al-lamaḥāt*. Edited by Emile Maalouf. Beirut: Dār al-Nahār, 1969.

———. *The Philosophy of Illumination*. Edited and translated by John Walbridge and Hossein Ziai. Provo, UT: Brigham Young University Press, 1999.

al-Taftāzānī, Saʿd al-Dīn. *Sharḥ al-Maqāṣid*. Edited by ʿAbd al-Raḥmān ʿUmayra. Beirut: ʿĀlam al-Kutub, 1998.

———. *Tahdhīb al-mantiq wa-l-kalām*. Kuwait: Dār al-Ḍiyāʾ, 2017.

Tellkamp, Jorg, and Luis Xavier Lopez Farjeat. *Philosophical Psychology in Medieval Arabic and Latin Aristotelianism*. Paris: Vrin, 2013.

al-Tūnisī, ʿAbd al-ʿAzīz Ibn Bazīza. *al-Isʿād fī sharḥ al-Irshād*. Kuwait: Dār al-Ḍiyāʾ, 2014.

al-Ṭūsī, Naṣīr al-Dīn. *Talkhīṣ al-Muḥaṣṣal*. Edited by ʿAbd Allāh Nūrānī. Tehran: Dānishgāh-i Makgīl, bā hamkārī-i Dānishgāh-i Ṭihrān, 1359.

Ueberweg, Friedrich. *System of Logic and History of Logical Doctrines*. Translated by Thomas Lindsay. London: Longmans, Green and Co., 1871.

Vasiliev, Nicolai. 'Imaginary (Non-Aristotelian) Logic'. *Logique & Analyse* 182 (2003): 127–63.

Vignaux, Paul. *Nominalisme au XIVe siècle*. Paris: Librairie J. Vrin, Conférence Albert-Le-Grand, 1948.

Weinberg, Julius. *Nicolaus of Autrecourt: A Study in 14th-Century Thought*. Princeton, NJ: Princeton University Press, 1948.